Conserving Water:
The Untapped Alternative

Sandra Postel

Worldwatch Paper 67
September 1985

Sections of this paper may be reproduced in magazines and news-papers with acknowledgment to Worldwatch Institute. The views expressed are those of the author and do not necessarily represent those of Worldwatch Institute and its directors, officers, or staff.

©Copyright Worldwatch Institute, 1985
Library of Congress Catalog Card Number 85-51713
ISBN 0-916468-67-4

Printed on recycled paper

Table of Contents

Introduction

5

Despite modern technology and feats of engineering, a secure water future for much of the world remains elusive. In Africa, prolonged drought, combined with a severe lack of developed water supplies, has triggered a crippling famine that some experts fear is but a prelude of things to come. Nowhere is water's crucial role in meeting basic human needs more evident. Yet water planners in many corners of the world—in humid climates as well as dry, in affluent societies as well as poor ones—are projecting that within two decades water supplies will fall short of needs. In the spring of 1985, officials in the eastern United States declared a drought emergency, asking millions of residents to curtail non-essential water uses, and in some cases rationing supplies, to avoid a critical shortage of drinking water.

Historically, water management has focused on water development—building dams, reservoirs, and diversion canals—to supply water wherever and in whatever amounts desired. Governments often built and financed large water projects to encourage agricultural and economic expansion. In the United States, for example, the 1902 Reclamation Act aimed to settle the western frontier by offering family farmers cheap water and power. The Act established a separate agency, the Bureau of Reclamation, explicitly charged with developing the West's rivers for irrigation and later for hydropower. Since

sincerely thank Cynthia Pollock for her research assistance, Susan Norris for her production assistance, and Mohamed El-Ashry, Andrea Fella, Marvin Jensen, Philip Metzger, Rick Piltz, David Pimentel, R. Neil Sampson, and Lee Wilson for their helpful comments on early drafts of the manuscript.

6

1902, hundreds of dams have been erected, and the Bureau has buil or authorized more than 160 irrigation projects. Collectively, they supply water to about one-quarter of the West's irrigated land.[1]

Viewed as a key to economic growth and prosperity, water develop ment in much of the world has expanded virtually unchecked. Where individuals drilled their own wells, pumping was regulated mini mally, if at all. Cities and farms sprawled across virtual deserts, anc water was brought to them. Soaring demands were met by ever large dam and diversion projects. Planners often projected future wate needs without considering whether available supplies could sus tainably meet them. Rarely did the notion of adapting to a limitec supply enter into planning scenarios.

Today's water institutions—the policies and laws, government agen cies, and planning and engineering practices that shape patterns o water use—are steeped in a supply-side management philosophy n longer appropriate to solving today's water problems. Aquifer deple tion, falling water tables, and streamflows diminished to ecologicall damaging levels are increasingly widespread. Though the con ventional approach of continuously expanding supplies may worl when water is abundant, it is not well suited for an era of growin scarcity, damage to the environment, and capital constraints.

By increasing water productivity—the benefit gained from each lite used—food production, industrial output, and cities can expan without a parallel increase in water demands. Investments in wate efficiency, recycling, and conservation can increasingly yield mor usable water per dollar than can conventional water supply projects But their potential is severely undermined by pricing policies an water laws that encourage inefficiency and waste. Removing thes institutional barriers is crucial in order to expand the many ne water-conserving methods now in limited use. Only by managin water demand, rather than ceaselessly striving to meet it, is ther hope for a truly secure and sustainable water future.

> "Only by managing water demand,
> rather than ceaselessly striving to meet it,
> is there hope for a truly secure
> and sustainable water future."

The Productivity Frontier

A look at some key water trends drives home the need to redirect water policy and planning. In several of the world's major crop producing regions, water use exceeds sustainable levels, potentially limiting future food production. Water tables are falling beneath one-quarter of the irrigated cropland in the United States. In the five states where levels are dropping most pervasively—Arizona, Kansas, New Mexico, Oklahoma, and Texas—net irrigated area declined between 1978 and 1982 by 678,000 hectares, or 14 percent.[2] (One hectare equals 2.47 acres.) Depletion of the Ogallala Aquifer, an essentially nonrenewable groundwater supply, threatens the agricultural economy of the U.S. High Plains, where 40 percent of the country's grain-fed beef are raised. Pumping in the Texas plains accounts for nearly 70 percent of the Ogallala's depletion so far and has diminished that region's supply by about a fourth.[3]

Trends in other major crop-producing regions are equally disturbing. About half of the Soviet Union's irrigated area is in the central Asian republics and southern Kazakhstan in the southwestern part of the country. Their fertile soils and sunny, warm climate make these regions ideal for expanding crop production, but lack of water severely limits this potential. In dry years, virtually the entire flow of the area's two primary rivers is already used. Little remains either to expand irrigated crop production or to supply the burgeoning population of this largely Moslem territory, which now totals more than 25 million. In China, a water deficit is building on the North Plain, which accounts for about a quarter of the value of that nation's crop output. Near Beijing, groundwater use exceeds the sustainable supply by a fourth, and water tables are dropping as much as two meters per year.[4]

These regions stand out because of their prominence in the world food economy, but they are not the only areas with water problems. Many coastal communities worldwide are battling threats of salt water intruding into their drinking water supply. Land has subsided in Mexico City, Beijing, California's Central Valley, the Texas coast, and elsewhere from overpumping and subsequent compaction of

8

underlying aquifers. In recent years, millions of urban residents in such climatically diverse areas as Newark, New Jersey; Corpus Christi, Texas; Managua, Nicaragua; and Tianjin, China, have had their household water rationed because of supply shortfalls. Perhaps most alarming of all, population continues to grow fastest in some of the world's most water-short regions. In Kenya, even if rainfall stays at its historical level, water supplies per person may drop by half within 17 years, simply because of population growth.[5]

While these problems become more severe and pervasive, traditional solutions are becoming more difficult and costly to implement. In Western Europe, North America, and Australia, few affordable and acceptable sites remain for damming and diverting more river water and the era of large-scale, government-financed water development has largely ended. A 1983 report by the U.S. Congressional Budget Office flatly concluded that "the days of huge federal outlays for equally large water projects appear to be over."[6] Future projects will require that beneficiaries pay more of the costs, and in many cases the costs will be prohibitive. The U.S. Army Corps of Engineers, for example, examined the possibility of diverting water from mid western rivers to farmers dependent on the diminishing Ogallala Aquifer, and found that the costs would be several times higher than what farmers could profitably pay.[7] With government support waning, large new water projects are unlikely to save irrigated farming in such areas of limited supply.

Both China and the Soviet Union are planning river diversion projects of unprecedented scale to augment supplies in their water-short food-producing regions. The Chinese scheme would divert water from the Chang Jiang (Yangtze) River 1,150 kilometers northward to the North Plain. The Soviets are preparing detailed engineering designs for a 2,500-kilometer diversion of Siberian rivers south into Central Asia. Yet these projects are costly and environmentally risky ways to increase and stabilize crop production. The Siberian diversion is projected to cost a daunting $37 billion. In dry years, it could deplete west Siberian streamflows by a fifth, reducing the biological productivity of floodplains and eliminating large areas of fish spawning and feeding habitat. Scientists have speculated about potential climatic changes from the reduction of river flows into Arctic waters.

"Since 1974, irrigated area overlying
the Texas portion of the Ogallala Aquifer
has dropped by more than
576,000 hectares, or 24 percent."

though Soviet experts maintain that no such dramatic alteration would occur from the first phase of the scheme. Nonetheless, as U.S. geographer Philip Micklin points out, the project is so large and complex that unforeseeable consequences are unavoidable "no matter how carefully planned, implemented, and operated (it) may be."[8]

Energy costs are a new, but growing constraint on water development. Water naturally seeks the most energy-efficient path to the sea, flowing by gravity in stream channels or through the pores and fractures of underground aquifers. Diverting water from its natural course requires energy in ever greater amounts as the scale, distance, or depth of diversions increase. China's diversion project, for example, will require several dozen pumping stations with a total installed capacity of about 1,000 megawatts—equal to one large nuclear plant or two large coal plants.[9]

The oil price increases of the seventies dramatically altered the economics of water supply and use. For U.S. farmers pumping their own irrigation water, the cost of energy rose from $530 million in 1974 to nearly $1.9 billion in 1980.[10] Rising energy prices, especially when combined with falling water tables, can increase irrigation costs to prohibitive levels. In the Texas plains, where water levels in some areas have dropped 50 meters over the last four decades, production costs have increased far faster than crop prices, forcing farmers to cease irrigation. Since 1974, irrigated area overlying the Texas portion of the Ogallala Aquifer has dropped by more than 576,000 hectares, or 24 percent.[11]

Though difficult to trace and quantify, the environmental costs of intensive water development are also escalating. In Soviet Central Asia, irrigation demands have so reduced freshwater flows to the Aral Sea that the Sea's surface area has shrunk nearly 30 percent since 1960. Fisheries once important to the regional economy have virtually disappeared. Similarly, in the United States, the diversion of California rivers and streams to supply farms and growing cities in the state's drier south has completely desiccated one lake and reduced another's surface area by a third. Less dramatic, but no less important, is the loss of fish and other aquatic life as their habitats are destroyed by severely diminished streamflows. For the western

United States, biologists recommend that depletions not exceed 40 percent of a stream's average annual flow. But in many river basins, depletions already total between 60 and 80 percent of streamflow. The consequences of such ecosystem destruction are largely uncalculated, but in some cases, probably irreversible.[12]

Wasteful use and poor management of water impose serious costs as well. Seepage from unlined irrigation canals, excessive watering of fields, and insufficient attention to drainage cause underground water levels to rise, eventually waterlogging the root zone of soils. In dry climates, water near the surface evaporates, leaving soils laden with a damaging layer of salts—a process known as salinization. Together waterlogging and salinization sterilize 1 million to 1.5 million hectares of cropland each year.[13]

Collectively, these factors—pervasive depletion and overuse of water supplies, the high capital cost of new large water projects, rising pumping costs, and worsening ecological damage—call for a shift in the way water is valued, used, and managed. If food production is to keep pace with expanding food needs, attention must turn to increasing water productivity in agriculture. Sustaining economic growth and supplying growing cities will require recycling, reusing, and conserving water to get more production out of existing supplies.

Most Third World countries have not developed their water sources as extensively as industrial countries have, and they face some special challenges in an era of scarce and costly water. Third World economies are still largely agrarian, and irrigated agriculture claims 85-90 percent of their developed water sources. Supplying an expanding urban and industrial base while meeting the food needs of growing populations will require much additional water. But these nations now confront far greater capital and energy constraints to water development than did those undergoing industrialization earlier this century. Few can afford to double water withdrawals within two decades, as, for example, the United States did between 1950 and 1970.[14] Only by building water efficiency into farms, factories, and growing urban areas can Third World countries prevent the constraints to water development from limiting agricultural output and economic growth.

Investing in Irrigation Efficiency

Since 1950, irrigated area worldwide has nearly tripled, now totaling about 270 million hectares. Water, fertilizer, and high-yielding seed varieties together fueled the Green Revolution that spread throughout South and East Asia during the sixties and seventies. In many Asian countries, irrigated lands now account for more than half of domestic food production. Today, one-third of the world's food is grown on just the 18 percent of cropland that is irrigated.[15]

11

In the drive to expand irrigation, however, comparatively little attention has been paid to the efficiency with which irrigation systems operate. Much water is lost as it is conveyed from reservoirs to farmlands, distributed among farmers, and applied to fields. Worldwide, the efficiency of irrigation systems is estimated to average only 37 percent. Some of this "lost" water returns to a stream or aquifer where it can be tapped again, provided the necessary infrastructure is available. But much is rendered unproductive or becomes severely degraded in quality as it picks up salts, pesticides, and toxic elements from the land.[16]

Besides accounting for about 70 percent of water withdrawals worldwide, agriculture consumes the largest share of most nations' water budgets. Whereas 90 percent or more of the water supplied to industries and homes is available for reuse, return flows from agriculture are often only half the initial withdrawal. The rest is consumed through evaporation and transpiration, which depletes the local water supply. Though water can be saved only by reducing consumption, reducing withdrawals—whether they are consumed or not—can make a given reservoir or aquifer supply last longer or serve a larger area. Raising irrigation efficiency by 10 percent in the Indus region of Pakistan, for example, could provide enough water to irrigate an additional 2 million hectares.[17] (Throughout this paper, the terms water withdrawal, use, and demand are used interchangeably; consumption is distinguished.)

Most farmers still irrigate the way their predecessors did 5,000 years ago—by flooding or channeling water through parallel furrows. Water flows by gravity across a gently sloping field, seeping into the soil along the way. These gravity systems (also called surface systems) are typically the least expensive to install and by far the mos common method in use today. Unfortunately, most fail to distribute water evenly. Farmers must often apply an excessive amount of water to ensure that enough reaches plants situated on higher ground or or the far side of the field. Some areas receive more water than the crops can use, and the excess percolates out of the root zone or simply runs off the field.[18]

Because of these problems, many gravity systems are less than 5(percent efficient: only half the water applied to the field actually benefits the crops. Yet a number of practices can greatly improve thei performance. Probably the most universally applicable is leveling the land so that water gets distributed more evenly. To sufficiently water crops sitting just 3 centimeters higher than the surrounding surface, farmers may have to apply as much as 40 percent more water to the entire field. Precise leveling can thus greatly reduce water needs, besides alleviating waterlogging, curbing erosion, and raising crop yields. It can be done with traditional equipment—a tractor or draf animals pulling a soil scraper and land plane—but most farmers wil require training and assistance in carrying out the initial field surveys and leveling operations. In recent years, farmers in the United States and elsewhere have begun to use lasers to guide the leveling process, which can raise the efficiency of surface systems to as high as 9(percent.[19]

Farmers can also reduce water losses by capturing and recycling water that would otherwise run off the field. This typically requires constructing a pond to collect and store the runoff, and installing pumps to return the water to the head of the field. Some U.S. states now require these tailwater recycling systems, and for many farmers they pay for themselves in reduced energy costs. Especially where irrigation water is drawn from great depths, the energy needed to recycle the runoff is usually less than that needed to pump new supplies from the aquifer.[20]

Researchers in Texas have recently devised a technique called "surge" irrigation that shows great promise for improving gravity systems. Usually water is released in a continuous stream until it has spread across the field, but the surge method releases water at specific intervals. The initial wetting seals the soil somewhat, allowing the next application to advance more quickly down the field. This surging effect reduces percolation losses at the head and distributes water more uniformly. Though this principle could likely be applied in simple farming systems, surge units developed for the U.S. market include a valve and timer that automatically release water at established intervals. Field tests indicate that surge irrigation reduces water and energy use by 10-40 percent. For farmers in the Texas plains, these savings would typically pay back the initial investment (about $33 per hectare) within three years.[21]

13

Over the last two decades, much new land has been brought under irrigation with a variety of high-pressure sprinkler designs. In some areas, farmers have used them to irrigate hilly and marginal lands unsuitable for gravity methods. Sprinkler irrigation accounts for virtually all of the net increase in irrigated area in the United States between 1960 and the early eighties, and today sprinklers are used on about 35-40 percent of U.S. irrigated land. The most common design is the center pivot, in which a horizontal sprinkler arm circles around a fixed point. Each covering about 50 hectares, center pivots now irrigate much of the U.S. High Plains with water drawn from the Ogallala Aquifer. Saudi Arabia has also adopted the technology in its drive for self-sufficiency in grain production. Some 12,000 center pivots have been installed in this desert nation over the last few years.[22]

Sprinklers tend to irrigate more uniformly than gravity systems, and efficiencies typically average about 70 percent. But especially in windy, dry areas, much water can be lost to evaporation. A new method, known as LEPA—for low-energy precision application— offers substantial improvements over conventional designs. Rather than spraying water high into the air, the LEPA method delivers water closer to the crops by means of drop tubes extending vertically from the sprinkler arm. When used in conjunction with water-conserving land preparation methods, LEPA irrigation can achieve efficiencies as high as 98 percent. Since the system operates at low pressure, energy requirements may drop by 20-30 percent.[23]

A key advantage of the LEPA technology is its suitability for retro-fitting existing sprinklers, including the common center pivot. For many center-pivot irrigators, a LEPA retrofit would pay for itself in reduced pumping costs within 5-7 years. Many farmers in northwestern Texas have already converted their systems. Irrigation specialists from Australia and Israel have studied the Texas design, and farmers in those countries are now operating similar systems. If widely adopted, LEPA irrigation could achieve substantial water savings at a reasonable cost. Upgrading all the center pivots in the High Plains, for example, could reduce pumping by as much as 2.2 billion cubic meters annually and help slow the Ogallala Aquifer's depletion.[24]

For fruits, vegetables, and orchard crops, a group of thrifty irrigation techniques collectively known as micro-irrigation has rapidly expanded over the last decade. The most common micro-method is drip (also known as trickle) irrigation, in which a network of porous or perforated piping, installed on or below the soil surface, delivers water directly to the crops' roots. This keeps evaporation and seepage losses extremely low. To sufficiently water the same crop, drip systems may apply 20-25 percent less water to the field than conventional sprinklers and 40-60 percent less than simple gravity systems. An important feature, especially for arid lands, is that drip appears better suited for irrigating with brackish water. The fairly constant level of moisture maintained in the root zone helps prevent salt concentrations from rising to yield-reducing levels.[25]

Although the principles behind drip irrigation date back more than a century, the emergence of inexpensive plastic following World War II spurred the technology's commercial development. By the mid-seventies, a half dozen countries—Australia, Israel, Mexico, New Zealand, South Africa, and the United States—were irrigating substantial areas by drip methods, and drip area worldwide totaled about 56,600 hectares. Since then its use has steadily spread. (See Table 1.) Israel now waters 73,200 hectares by drip methods, up from 6,000 just a decade ago. Together drip systems and micro-sprinklers water nearly half the nation's total irrigated area. Along with effective management, use of these micro-irrigation methods accounts for much of Israel's impressive efficiency gains, including a 20 percent drop in 14

Table 1: Use of Micro-Irrigation in Leading Countries[1]

Country	1974	1981-82[2]
	(hectares)	
United States	29,060	185,300
Israel	6,070	81,700
South Africa	3,480	44,000
France	—	22,000
Australia	10,120	20,050
Soviet Union	—	11,200
Italy	—	10,300
China	—	8,040
Cyprus	160	6,600
Mexico	6,470	5,500
All Other	1,010	21,970
Total	56,370	416,660

[1]Includes primarily surface and subsurface drip methods and micro-sprinklers. [2]See text for selected, more up-to-date estimates.

Sources: 1974 estimates from Don Gustafson, "Drip Irrigation in the World—State of the Art," in *Israqua '78: Proceedings of the International Conference on Water Systems and Applications* (Tel Aviv: Israel Centre of Waterworks Appliances, 1978); 1981-82 estimates adapted from J.S. Abbott, "Micro Irrigation—World Wide Usage," *Bulletin of the International Commission on Irrigation and Drainage,* January 1984.

years in the average volume of water applied to each irrigated hectare. In the United States, drip systems still comprise a negligible share of total irrigated area. But their use greatly expanded over the last decade—from 29,000 hectares in 1974 to more than 226,000 hectares in 1983. California accounts for nearly half the U.S. total, and Florida for about a fifth. Today micro-irrigation systems—including drip and micro-sprinklers—water more than 475,000 hectares worldwide, an eightfold increase since the mid-seventies.[26]

Despite impressive expansion, drip irrigation accounts for less than 1 percent of total irrigated area worldwide. With capital costs in the range of $2,200-$3,500 per hectare, it has so far attracted mainly growers of higher-valued orchard crops, grapes, and vegetables. Yet over the last few years, some cotton growers have turned to the technology. About 25,000 hectares of cotton are drip-irrigated in Israel, 42 percent of the nation's total crop. In the United States, more than 7,000 hectares of cotton are under drip irrigation, most of it in Arizona, and the Soviet Union has experimented with the method on 300 hectares of its cotton crop.[27]

Though new technologies can do much to reduce water withdrawals for agriculture, many are too costly and complex to benefit farmers in the Third World. Incorporating the principles behind these modern techniques into technologies affordable and appropriate for a Third World setting should be a high research priority. One method, for example, known as "pitcher irrigation," incorporates properties somewhat akin to drip systems. Vegetable or fruit seeds are planted around a baked earthen pitcher buried in the soil. Farmers fill the pitcher with water, which then gradually seeps through the porous walls into the root zone. As with drip systems, evaporation and water losses remain very low. Locally manufactured in many developing countries, the pitchers offer an inexpensive and efficient water-delivery method. Experiments in India in the early seventies showed pitcher irrigation to work well with pumpkins and melons, and more recently, a local association of farmers in the state of Piani, Brazil, began using the technique.[28]

With investment needs for new large-scale irrigation projects in the Third World averaging about $5,000 per hectare, most experts agree that near-term efforts should focus on increasing the efficiency of systems already in place. Better management alone could reduce water withdrawals for most surface canal systems by at least 10-15 percent, allowing new land to be brought under irrigation for a much lower cost than developing new supplies. The World Bank estimates, for example, that reducing from 50 to 30 percent the loss of water from systems supplying 13 million hectares in Pakistan would recapture for productive use a volume of water equal to that stored by three Tarbela Dams—the equivalent of a $9 billion investment.[29]

> "Most experts agree that near-term efforts in the Third World should focus on increasing the efficiency of irrigation systems already in place."

What constitutes "better management" varies from project to project. Typical problems include the large water losses resulting from canal seepage as water is conveyed from reservoirs to fields, poor mechanisms for distributing water among the farmers served by a particular project, and, at the farm level, lack of control over the timing and amount of water applied to fields. Consequently, often less land is irrigated than was originally planned in a project design, contributing to the low rate of return from many irrigation investments. Some farmers get too much water, while others get too little, and few apply water to their crops in optimal amounts. These shortcomings diminish not only the productivity of the water supply, but food production and farmers' livelihoods. An analysis of the Rajangana irrigation project in Sri Lanka, for example, found that farmers located near the tail-end of the system—and who therefore had last access to water in the irrigation canal—had average incomes one-fifth lower than those near the head, where the supply was plentiful. Despite ample application of fertilizer, rice yields from most farmers' fields were far below their potential.[30]

Only if farmers are assured of an adequate and reliable supply of water will they invest in other inputs that can boost productivity, such as fertilizer and high-yielding seeds. Many large canal systems now deliver water according to a rigid schedule that gives farmers little control over their supply. Robert Chambers of the University of Sussex cites farmers in Gujarat, India, who were willing to pay 7-9 times more for pumped groundwater than for canal water because the former was more reliable.[31] Since farmers ultimately use the water and know best what their system's problems are, their involvement in management decisions is crucial. Especially in government-run projects, some form of farmers' organization is necessary to make farmers' concerns and needs known to decision-makers in the irrigation bureaucracy. Such an organization also provides a mechanism for collecting fees to cover operation and maintenance costs, without which expensive irrigation works fall into disrepair.

Whatever the type of system used—flood or furrow, sprinklers, or drip methods—farmers can greatly increase their water efficiency on the farm by scheduling their irrigations to more closely coincide with

17

their crops' water needs. This requires periodically monitoring soil moisture and irrigating just before crops would become stressed by lack of water. Farmers with limited financial resources may do fairly well by extracting a soil sample from the appropriate depth and estimating moisture content by its consistency. If data on evapotranspiration and rainfall are available, growers can keep a water budget, irrigating when their calculations show that their crops will soon need more water.[32]

Many devices are available to measure soil moisture, of which gypsum blocks are probably the least costly and simplest to use. When buried in the root zone, the blocks (costing about $4 each) acquire a moisture content roughly equal to that of the surrounding soil. Electrodes embedded inside them are connected to a meter (costing about $100) that measures electrical resistance: the wetter the soil, the wetter the gypsum block, and the less it will impede an electrical current. When interpreted for the appropriate soil type, the meter reading tells the farmer how moist or dry the soil is. On test plots of alfalfa and corn, irrigation scheduling using gypsum blocks led to, respectively, a 14 and 27 percent reduction in water applications compared to neighboring control plots. One tomato grower estimated that the method could cut the number of irrigations needed during the growing season from his usual five or seven to three, with a probable 20 percent reduction in water use.[33]

Greater efforts should be made to train farmers in the use of irrigation scheduling methods appropriate to their mode of production. Including such training in the agricultural extension programs now operating in many countries could help spread the benefits of these water-conserving techniques. In the United States, scheduling services are offered through various government agencies, universities, water districts, and private consultants. Programs are now under way in several states, including California, Nebraska, and Michigan.[34]

Especially where irrigation systems are extremely inefficient, as is the case in much of the Third World today, substantial water productivity gains can be made for a small price. A case in point is the Claro River Valley in Chile, situated about 100 kilometers south of Santiago, and one of the nation's prime agricultural areas. Practically no rain falls

**"An investment in irrigation efficiency
is also an investment in
the productivity of crops and soils."**

during the valley's 6-8 month dry season, and farming has required construction of expensive irrigation projects. Investigations in the mid-seventies showed that irrigation efficiencies were averaging only about 20 percent, drainage was poor, and nutrients were being leached out of the root zone—all contributing to low crop yields.[35]

19

The Chilean Ministry of Civil Works, aided by technical experts from West Germany and the Catholic University of Chile, launched a study to determine the benefits of some simple and inexpensive irrigation improvements. On selected plots, the research group modified traditional furrow and flood irrigation methods to get a more even distribution of water thoughout the field. Soil moisture was monitored, and crops were irrigated when moisture in the root zone had been depleted by about half. For a total annual cost of only $25-$30 per hectare, the irrigation improvements led to some dramatic results. (See Table 2.) Half of the controlled irrigations achieved efficiencies of 60 percent or greater, whereas only 15 percent did in the uncontrolled fields. Yields of alfalfa doubled compared to those in the unimproved plots, potato yields were two-thirds higher, and barley yields 43 percent higher. Water productivity—measured as output per unit of water applied to the field—was boosted 30-136 percent for several key crops.

Which of these myriad technologies and practices proves practical and economical will vary from place to place. But if given sufficient incentives, most farmers could cut their water withdrawals by 10-40 percent without reducing crop production. Experience shows that an investment in irrigation efficiency is usually also an investment in the productivity of crops and soils. With better water management, yields often increase, erosion is reduced, and soils are less likely to become waterlogged or sapped of nutrients. Encouraging more widespread adoption of water-saving methods would help sustain irrigated agriculture where water supplies are diminishing, curb ecological damage to overtaxed rivers and streams, and help the growing number of farmers faced with rising water costs stay in business.

Table 2: Water Productivity Gains in Claro River Valley, Chile

Crop	Average Yield		Average Water Use		Change in Water Pro- ductivity[2]
	Without Improve- ments	With Improve- ments[1]	Without Improve- ments	With Improve- ments[1]	
	(thousand kilograms/ hectare)		(thousand cubic meters/hectare)		(percent)
Alfalfa	5.10	10.14	18.07	15.47	+136
Barley	2.37	3.39	7.96	5.80	+ 93
Beans	1.03	1.03	10.40	7.80	+ 30
Potatoes	2.93	4.80	11.70	8.80	+120

[1]Annual cost for improvements did not exceed $30 per hectare. [2]Water productivity was calculated from the authors' figures for comparative yields and water savings and is measured in kilograms of crop output per cubic meter of water used.

Source: Gaston Mahave and Jorge Dominguez, "Experiments at Farm Level to Intro- duce Technology in Irrigation: Its Influence on Production and Water Re- sources," in Brazilian National Committee, *Transactions of the 1st Regional Pan-American Conference*, Vol. 1, Salvador (Bahia), Brazil, October 1984.

New Cropping Patterns

Though the spread of irrigation has fostered a tremendous surge in crop production over the last generation, more than 80 percent of the world's cropland is still watered only by rainfall. These lands produce two-thirds of the global harvest and are the source of subsistence diets for many growing Third World populations. Some of this land can and will, in time, be brought under irrigation. But given the high cost of new irrigation projects—often $10,000-$15,000 per hectare in much of Africa—expanding irrigation may in many cases not be a feasible near-term solution to raising food production.[36] Effective water management is as crucial to increasing crop yields in non-irrigated agriculture as it is in irrigated agriculture. Yet with irrigation occupying center stage in recent decades, the potential to improve water productivity on rain-fed farmland has been largely neglected.

"More than 80 percent of
the world's cropland is still
watered only by rainfall."

Rain-fed farming (often called dryland farming in arid and semi-arid regions) is inherently a risky enterprise. Regardless of what an historical rainfall record may show, dryland farmers have no guarantee that rain will sufficiently water their crops throughout the growing season. In a dry year, the quality of water management in dryland production can mean the difference between a field of withered crops and a successful harvest. Capturing and retaining rainwater on the land, reducing the amount of water lost to evaporation, and selecting crops suited to regional rainfall patterns are the keys to enhancing productivity. According to U.S. Department of Agriculture researchers B.A. Stewart and Earl Burnett, these components of sustainable dryland farming have been known for centuries, but "progress in adapting them to specific areas and situations has been slow."[37]

21

Wherever water is the only factor limiting crop production, a crop's yield varies directly with the amount of water available for evapotranspiration. Beyond a minimum requirement, for example, each additional millimeter of water transpired by a sorghum plant might correspond with an additional 15 kilograms of dry plant matter. By increasing the amount of moisture stored in the root zone, farmers can thus increase their crop yields.[38]

Making effective use of the fallow period—the time between one crop's harvest and the next one's planting—can substantially increase soil moisture storage. While fields lie idle, rainwater accumulates in the root zone, helping fill the gap between the next crop's water requirements and the amount of rain that falls during its growing season. Researchers have found that yields under well-planned crop-fallow rotations can increase dramatically compared with those under continuous cropping. In some cases, this boost in yield may more than compensate for the fewer number of harvests. Yields of wheat, for example, have doubled or tripled after a year of fallow compared with continuous cropping.[39]

Conservation tillage, besides helping farmers cut energy costs and curb soil erosion, is among the most effective water-conservation practices. The crop residues left on the field after harvest trap rainwater, slow runoff, and reduce evaporation from the soil, thus increasing soil moisture storage. Studies of an irrigated wheat/dryland sorghum cropping system in Texas, for example, found that compared with two traditional tillage methods, conservation tillage (in this case, no-till) increased the amount of rainwater stored in the soil by 12 and 20 percent, respectively. Sorghum yields were 26 and 66 percent higher, for total water productivity gains of 16 and 35 percent.[40]

Another study in the southern High Plains found that both soil water storage and sorghum yields increased in proportion to the amount of residue left on the field during an 11-month fallow. (See Table 3.) With 8 tons of residue per hectare, 44 percent of the precipitation falling during the fallow was retained in the soil, compared with only 23 percent on fields cleared of residue. Moreover, sorghum yields on fields with the 8 tons of residue were double those on the cleared field—again, a tremendous gain as a result of conserving natural rainfall. Conservation tillage involves some tradeoffs, however, including an increased risk of groundwater contamination from the greater use of agriculture chemicals. In much of the Third World, its benefits for crop production would also have to be weighed against other uses of crop residues, such as feeding livestock or burning as fuel.

Using rainfall effectively is as important while crops are growing as during the fallow period. As many as 4,000 years ago, farmers practiced techniques known as "runoff agriculture," a form of water harvesting in which rainwater is captured and channeled to fields to provide enough water for crops to grow in an otherwise hostile environment. These methods allowed some ancient farming cultures to thrive where annual rainfall averaged only 100 millimeters (4 inches), and became widely used throughout the Middle East, North Africa, China, India, northwest Mexico, and the American Southwest. About a quarter century ago, researchers in Israel's Negev Desert revived interest in these techniques. If combined with today's knowledge of crop water needs and local rainfall patterns, modern variants of runoff agriculture could increase dryland production in arid regions and greatly lessen the risk of crop failure.[41]

One promising method for small-scale subsistance crop production is micro-catchment farming. The terrain around each cultivated plant is

Table 3: Effects of Conservation Tillage on Water Storage and Sorghum Yields in the Southern U.S. High Plains

Amount of Residue Left on the Field	Share of Fallow-Period Precipitation Stored in the Soil	Sorghum Yield
(tons/hectare)	(percent)	(kilograms/hectare)
0	23	1,780
1	31	2,410
2	31	2,600
4	36	2,980
8	44	3,680
12	46	3,990

Sources: B.A. Stewart and Earl Burnett, "Water Conservation Technology in Rainfed and Dryland Agriculture," paper presented at the International Conference on Food and Water, College Station, Texas, May 26-30, 1985. Original data is from P.W. Unger, "Straw-Mulch Rate Effect on Soil Water Storage and Sorghum Yield," Soil Science Society of America Journal, Vol. 42, 1978.

shaped so that rainfall from a larger area gets directed to a small basin in which the plant grows. Water retained in the basin seeps through the soil, and the crop gets a greater supply than it otherwise would from rainfall alone. Experiments in the Negev indicate construction costs of only $10-$40 per hectare, depending on the catchment size needed to sufficiently supply the crop. Despite their applicability for labor-intensive, subsistence cropping systems, which characterizes much of Third World agriculture, micro-catchments are only in limited use. By the early seventies, the technique was applied in several countries, including Mexico, Botswana, India, Pakistan, Australia, and Afghanistan, but is in widespread use today only in the Mediterranean region. Since micro-catchments work especially well with tree crops, they could bolster reforestation efforts that combine production of food, fodder, and fuelwood—an urgent need, for example, in sub-Saharan Africa.[42]

Farmers in dry regions of the United States have in recent years adopted a practice known as "furrow diking," a variation of the micro-catchment technique. Mounds of soil constructed at periodic intervals across each furrow trap rainwater in small basins so that water infiltrates the soil rather than runs off the field. With the added moisture, yields of cotton and sorghum have increased as much as 25-30 percent over those on undiked fields. Though especially helpful to dryland farmers, the method is also useful on irrigated fields, where it helps retain both rainwater and costly irrigation water. Researchers in Texas estimate that 1.2 million hectares of Texas High Plains farmland are now furrow-diked for some portion of the year, and that in years of at least average rainfall, the practice may increase the value of the region's crop production by $87 million.[43]

As water becomes an increasing constraint to food production, more attention must be given to exploiting crop characteristics and selecting cropping systems that make optimum use of the water available. Crops vary, among other things, in their resistance to drought, their tolerance of salinity, the total amount of water they consume from planting to harvest, and the length of their growing season. (See Table 4.) In dryland production, for example, farmers can help secure a good harvest by setting the planting date of a crop so that its growing season corresponds with the maximum probability of it getting sufficient moisture. They can also switch to crops and farming techniques better suited to their particular growing conditions.

A crop's water requirements depend on a variety of climatic factors including temperature, humidity, and the amount of sunlight, as well as on the crop's physiology and the length of its growing season. In the U.S. High Plains, for example, a corn plant—which has a comparatively long growing season—needs about 660 millimeters of water from planting to harvest, while soybeans may be grown with 550, grain sorghum with 510, and winter wheat with 460.[44] If irrigation water is available and inexpensive, these variations do not generally influence regional cropping patterns. But as water scarcity and cost begin to constrain irrigated production, shifts with potentially far-reaching effects may occur.

In the U.S. High Plains, for example, corn irrigated with water from the Ogallala Aquifer has supplied much of the feed grain for the region's burgeoning cattle industry over the last few decades. Today

Table 4: Seasonal Water Consumption for Selected Crops, Southwestern United States

Crop	Water Consumption (millimeters)	Growing Season	Length of Growing Season (days)
Alfalfa	1,890	Feb.-Nov.	285
Grapefruit	1,220	Jan.-Dec.	360
Sugarbeets	1,090	Oct.-July.	300
Cotton	1,050	April-Nov.	225
Wheat	660	Nov.-May	210
Grain Sorghum	650	July-Oct.	120
Barley	640	Nov.-May	180
Potatoes	620	Feb.-June	120
Soybeans	560	June-Oct.	135
Broccoli	500	Sept.-Feb.	165
Carrots	420	Sept.-March	180
Lettuce	220	Sept.-Dec.	105

Source: L.J. Erie et al., *Consumptive Use of Water by Major Crops in the Southwestern United States* (Washington, D.C.: U.S. Department of Agriculture, 1982).

the High Plains produces roughly 40 percent of America's grain-fed beef. Rising pumping costs and diminishing well yields are forcing a growing number of farmers to switch from irrigated corn to crops that require less irrigation or that can be dryland-farmed, such as sorghum. Sorghum needs about a fifth less water than corn and has nearly the same feed value, but its yields are substantially lower. A long-term decline in production is inevitable in a region that has thrived on an unsustainable use of water. But the shift to less water-intensive cropping patterns will pose hardships for farmers, local economies, and possibly the nation's beef consumers. As agricultural economist Philip M. Raup says, "We have a fed beef economy that has become dangerously dependent on an exhaustible resource base."[45]

In regions prone to drought, or where water supplies are otherwise unreliable, crops less sensitive to water stress can help guard against devastating yield reductions. Among the common grains, corn and rice are highly sensitive to water deficits, whereas sorghum and wheat, for example, are comparatively tolerant. While both corn and sorghum would likely suffer yield reductions during a prolonged drought, corn yields would drop by a greater percentage, other things being equal.[46] Research directed at boosting the yields of drought-resistant crops could thus greatly benefit areas where irrigation is limited or unavailable, including much of Africa.

A graph of any crop's seasonal water consumption typically has a bell shape, starting out low when plants are young, reaching a peak at some point in the growing season, and tapering off as harvest approaches. In general, crops are more sensitive to water deficiencies during their flowering or reproductive stage than during their vegetative or ripening stages. For example, if corn's water needs are not met during its silking and tasseling period, yields can drop by half. Though sorghum, cotton, and soybeans are more drought-tolerant than corn, their yields also can fall by a third or more if stressed by lack of water at their critical growth stages.[47] Where lack of developed supplies makes full irrigation impossible, the limited water available could be used to irrigate crops during their most sensitive periods. Especially in the Third World, where minimizing crop water stress can help avert famine, training farmers to apply water at the most critical times for their particular crops—and making supplies available during those times—could greatly enhance food security.

Another exploitable crop characteristic of growing importance is salt tolerance. Barley, cotton, sorghum, soybeans, sugarbeets, and wheat are among the common crops at least moderately tolerant of salinity. This trait is especially useful for desert regions, such as the Middle East, where a large share of the extractable groundwater supply is quite salty. To conserve high-quality water for drinking, the Saudi Arabians frequently use water with a salt concentration exceeding 2,000 parts per million (ppm) to grow barley, sugar beets, cotton, spinach, asparagus, and date palms.[48] (For comparison, ocean water has a salinity of about 35,000 ppm; water with a salinity of 1,000 ppm or less is considered fresh; and the recommended limit for drinking water in the United States is 500 ppm.)

"If corn's water needs are not met
during its silking and tasseling period,
yields can drop by half."

Some scientists see a promising future for the commercial production
of halophytes—plants physiologically adapted to a salty environment. Researchers at the University of Arizona's Environmental Research Laboratory in Tucson have collected several thousand
halophyte specimens representing some 800 species. Of the small
portion screened so far, a number appear promising as providers of
livestock feed or plant oil. Chickens, for example, can tolerate feed
with a halophyte content of 10-20 percent. Of course, before any
halophyte crop is grown on a commercial scale, it must be proven
economical to seed, cultivate, harvest, and sell.[49]

27

Over the long term, water constraints could prompt the spread of
new crop varieties. One that has attracted some recent attention is
amaranth, a broad-leaved plant that produces an edible cereal-like
grain. Native to Mexico, Guatemala, the southwestern United States,
and the Andean highlands of South America, amaranth is a hearty,
drought-resistant crop that appears readily adaptable to new envi-
ronments. About 20 farmers are growing it in the United States, and
some with several years experience see a potentially large role for the
crop in the High Plains. According to one Kansas grower, amaranth
weathered the recent dry years better than sorghum. However, given
its comparatively low yields and technical problems that make planting costly, amaranth will not supplant substantial acreages of the
common cereals without much additional research and
development.[50]

Recycling and Reuse

Most water supplies are taken from a river or an aquifer, used in a
factory or home, and then released as "wastewater" to the nearest
watercourse. As water demands increase, this approach easily over-
taxes water sources. Not only must large quantities of fresh water be
made available, but natural waterways are relied upon to dilute the
wastes discharged. After decades of this practice in industrial countries, widespread pollution made it clear that rivers and streams could
not assimilate the increasing tonnage of sewage and waste dumped
into them each year.

Municipal and industrial wastewater treatment not only protects the quality of rivers, streams, and aquifers, but sets the stage for water recycling and reuse. By using water several times, cities and industries can get more production out of each cubic meter, thereby lessening the need to develop new water supplies. Water pure enough to drink serves many functions that do not require such high quality. Much wastewater can therefore be used again within a given factory, home, or business (usually called recycling), or collected from one or more sites, treated, and redistributed to a new site (called reuse).

In the United States, manufacturing industries took in some 49 billion cubic meters of water in 1978, the last year for which a comprehensive survey is available. On average, each cubic meter was used 3.42 times before being discharged, eliminating the need to withdraw 120 billion cubic meters from the nation's water sources. More than 80 percent of all the water used in U.S. manufacturing is in just four industries—paper, chemicals, petroleum, and primary metals—and each has fairly steadily increased its water recycling rate over the last few decades. (See Table 5.) Each cubic meter supplied to paper mills, for example, is now used an average of 7.2 times, and for the paper industry as a whole, the average recycling rate has climbed from 2.38 to 5.3. Petroleum refineries recycle water about 7 times, chemical product manufacturers about 2.9 times, and primary metal industries—dominated by steelmaking—about 1.9 times.

Despite impressive progress, water recycling's potential in manufacturing has barely been tapped. Many industrial pollution-control processes recycle water by design. Also, because wastewaters must be treated to a high quality to meet environmental regulations, recycling partially treated water within a plant becomes more economical than paying the high costs of treating discharges to the levels required. As pollution control standards get more stringent, recycling rates tend to increase. The projected 1985 rates (in Table 5) are likely overestimates since compliance with pollution control requirements has lagged. But by the year 2000, the recycling rates in both the primary metals and paper industries are expected to rise to about 12, in chemicals to 28, and in petroleum to more than 30, with an average for all manufacturing industries of 17. If these levels are reached, total water withdrawals for manufacturing in the year 2000—taking into

"As pollution control standards
get more stringent, recycling
rates tend to increase."

Table 5: Water-Recycling Rates in U.S. Manufacturing Industries,
1954-78, with Projections for 1985 and 2000

Year	Paper and Allied Products	Chemicals and Allied Products	Petroleum and Coal Products	Primary Metal Industries	All Manu- facturing
1954	2.38	1.60	3.33	1.29	1.82
1959	3.12	1.61	4.38	1.53	2.16
1964	2.66	1.98	4.41	1.46	2.13
1968	2.90	2.10	5.08	1.55	2.31
1973	3.37	2.66	6.36	1.79	2.89
1978	5.30	2.89	6.98	1.91	3.42
1985	6.64	13.19	18.33	5.99	8.63
2000	11.84	28.03	32.73	12.31	17.08

Sources: U.S. Department of Commerce, Bureau of the Census, *Water Use in Manu-facturing* (Washington, D.C.: U.S. Government Printing Office, 1981). Projections for 1985 and 2000 from Culp et al., *Water Reuse and Recycling: Evaluation of Needs and Potential*, Vol. 1 (Washington, D.C.: U.S. Department of the Interior, 1979).

account expected economic growth—will be 45 percent less than they were in 1978.[51]

Some industrial plants are already operating close to these recycling levels, attesting to the technical feasibility of attaining them. An Armco steel mill in Kansas City, Missouri, which manufactures steel bars from recycled ferrous scrap, draws into the mill only 9 cubic meters of water per ton of steel produced, compared with as much as 100-200 cubic meters per ton in many other steel plants. Besides cutting its total water needs by using recycled iron scrap rather than new metal in its production, the Armco plant uses each liter of water 16 times before releasing it, after final treatment, to the river. One paper mill in Hadera, Israel, requires only 12 cubic meters of water per ton of paper, whereas many of the world's mills use 7-10 times this amount. In water-short regions of the Soviet Union, six oil refineries are now using closed water systems; wastewater is continuously treated and reused so that none is discharged.[52]

The economics of industrial water recycling vary greatly from one site to another. In paper-making, for example, water is used in virtually every step, and its quality may greatly affect the quality of the final product. A mill turning out newsprint or paper towels can typically recycle more of its process water without compromising its product than can a mill producing white bond paper.[53]

In deciding how much to recycle, any industry weighs the combined costs of getting water and treating it prior to disposal with those of treating wastewaters for reuse within the plant. In most industries, recycling offsets its costs by recovering valuable materials, such as nickel and chrome from plating operations, silver from photographic processing, and fiber from paper-making. As water and wastewater treatment costs rise, recycling thus begins to pay. One California paper mill, for example, when required by state authorities to curb its release of pollutants into the Pacific Ocean, found that internally treating and recycling its wastewater was the least expensive way to meet the state's requirements. Water use was cut by 15 percent, and by annually reclaiming $548,000 worth of fiber that otherwise would be discarded, the system essentially pays for itself.[54]

If encouraged, industrial recycling can make a dramatic difference in a region or nation's water use and quality. In Sweden, strict pollution control requirements have led to widespread adoption of recycling in its pulp and paper industry, which accounts for 80 percent of the nation's industrial water use. Between the early sixties and late seventies, the industry halved its water use while doubling production, a fourfold increase in water efficiency. Not only were Sweden's rivers and streams much cleaner, the nation's total water use in the mid-seventies was only half the level projected a decade earlier.[55]

Compelled by its chronically short water supply, Israel sets water use standards for each industry. Factories are allocated only as much water as necessary to achieve their production targets. As new technologies are developed, the standards become more stringent. This forced efficiency has greatly increased water productivity in Israeli

Table 6: Water Productivity in Selected Israeli Industries, 1962-75

Industry	Value of Output Per Cubic Meter		Change
	1962	1975	
	(constant Israeli pounds)		(percent)
Metal Products	153.8	400.0	+ 160
Food	84.7	142.9	+ 69
Nonmetallic Minerals	79.4	250.0	+ 215
Textiles	66.7	125.0	+ 87
Wood Products	55.2	500.0	+ 806
Chemicals	35.3	100.0	+ 183
Paper Products	15.7	62.5	+ 298
Mining & Quarrying	6.8	18.2	+ 168
All Industries	49.7	128.2	+ 158

Source: S. Arlosoroff, "Policy and Means for the Achievement of Efficient Water Use in Israel," in *Israqua '78: Proceedings of the International Conference on Water Systems and Applications* (Tel-Aviv: Israel Centre of Waterworks Appliances, 1978).

industries. (See Table 6.) In less than 15 years, the inflation-adjusted value of industrial output per cubic meter of water used rose 2.6 times.[56]

Along with industrial recycling, reusing municipal supplies can reduce demands for high-quality water. Most of the world's cities have opted for centralized sewer systems that collect household and commercial wastewater via an extensive piping network, transport it to a central treatment plant, and then dispose of it to the ocean, a bay, or a nearby river. Treatment progresses in stages, starting with physical processes that remove solids, followed by biological methods that reduce organic matter, and then by chemical treatment for further upgrading. The level of treatment given usually depends on the water quality controls in effect. In the United States, federal laws stipulate that all wastewaters be treated at least through the second stage before being released to the environment. Such treatment generally makes the water suitable for use where people will not directly contact it, such as industrial cooling or irrigating pasture. More extensive treatment can make the water safe for a wide variety of other functions.

By setting and enforcing pollution control standards and encouraging reuse of existing supplies, policymakers can lessen the need to import costly new supplies from a distant river basin, or to overexploit underground aquifers. Especially in many Third World cities, incorporating water reuse into plans for water and wastewater services can help meet rising household water demands, which in some cities may double or triple over the next two decades. In the Valley of Mexico, for example, 4 out of every 10 liters pumped from local aquifers are not replaced by recharge. Portions of the land already are sinking from the overpumping, and few affordable options exist to import more fresh water. In the region known as the Federal District, which includes about 70 percent of the Mexico City metropolitan area population, treated wastewater supplies about 4 percent of current water use, mainly watering public parks and filling recreational lakes. Planners have set the year 2000 as a target for reusing 17 percent of the wastewater generated in the District, which, if accomplished, would meet about 12 percent of projected water demands.[57]

In Israel, where virtually no freshwater supplies remain untapped, all new demands will be met by treating and reusing wastewater. Reclaimed water will replace one-fourth or more of the fresh water currently used in agriculture, releasing high-quality supplies for growing cities and industries. By the year 2000, treated wastewater is expected to supply 16 percent of the nation's total water needs, up from 4 percent in 1980.[58]

Israel's largest reuse scheme is in the Dan Region, which encompasses the metropolitan area of Tel Aviv, Jaffa, and six other cities with a total population of just over 1 million. (See Table 7.) After biological and chemical treatment, the wastewater is directed to spreading basins where it percolates to an underlying aquifer that is isolated from other underground sources of drinking water. Besides getting added treatment as it seeps through the soil, the water is

Table 7: Selected Sites of Large-Scale Water Reuse

Site/Region	Volume (cubic meters/day)	Purpose
Bethlehem Steel Co., Baltimore, Maryland	401,200	Cooling; steel processing
Dan Region, Israel	274,000	Groundwater recharge and storage; irrigation
Los Angeles and Orange Counties, California	200,000	Landscape irrigation; industrial cooling; groundwater recharge; control of sea-water intrusion
Wroclaw, Poland	170,000	Irrigating crops; groundwater recharge
Muskegan Co., Michigan	159,000	Irrigating crops
Mexico City Metropolitan Area	155,500	Irrigating public parks; recreational lakes
Riyadh, Saudi Arabia	120,000	Irrigation; petroleum refining
Nevada Power Company Las Vegas, Nevada	102,200	Power plant cooling
Kohtoh Industrial Water Works Tokyo, Japan	71,200	Supplying a variety of industries to alleviate groundwater overpumping

Sources: Mexico City and Poland examples from papers presented at *Water Reuse Symposium II*, 1981; Bethlehem Steel and Nevada Power examples cited in Donovan et al., *Guidelines for Water Reuse*; Tokyo citation from M. Sagoh, "Reuse of Water and Recycling," in *Proceedings of the International Water Conference*, Pittsburgh, Pennsylvania, Engineers' Society of Western Pennsylvania, 1982. See text for Israel and southern California references.

stored where little of it will evaporate. After a minimum of a hundred days, the water is recovered by wells and distributed, primarily for irrigation. The project's capacity is now about 274,000 cubic meters per day, and is expanding. Upon its completion, about 80 percent of the region's wastewater will be returned to productive use.[59]

In the United States, despite federal water quality laws that expressly encourage reuse, reclaimed wastewater comprises only 0.2 percent of total annual water use. Most communities have chosen the conventional treat-and-dispose types of systems. A survey in the late seventies showed that 536 reuse projects were under way, collectively using about 937 million cubic meters of treated wastewater annually. Over 60 percent of it was used for irrigating crops, parks, and landscapes, a third for industrial cooling and processing, and the remainder for recharging groundwater and various recreational functions.[60]

California, which leads the United States in the number of reuse projects, has promoted wastewater reclamation as an integral part of its water management plans. Based on extensive investigation into potential health effects, the state's Department of Health developed standards of quality for various uses of treated wastewater. Reuse for drinking has so far not been permitted. Standards are most strict for irrigating food crops, watering parks and playgrounds, and other activities where people are exposed to the wastewater. In 1978, a separate Office of Water Recycling was established specifically to promote reuse within the state. Grants and low-interest loans have been made available to local agencies to plan and construct reclamation projects. As a result of these initiatives, 380 individual sites are now supplied with reclaimed water (the late seventies' survey had identified 283), and collectively they return to productive use more than 271 million cubic meters of water annually—a volume equal to the yearly household needs of 1 million people.[61]

If fully exploited, water reuse could supply—at lower cost—as much additional water for southern California as would proposed expansions of the State Water Project, the complex of dams, reservoirs, and aqueducts that ships water from north to south. Two new dams and reservoirs proposed by state planners would increase supplies for southern cities by, respectively, 272 million cubic meters and 327 million cubic meters annually, while greater reclamation and reuse could add as much as 300 million cubic meters annually. Detailed calculations by economists at the Environmental Defense Fund show that the marginal cost of water supplied through greater reuse is, respectively, 14 percent and 31 percent less than that supplied by the two respective dam and diversion projects.[62]

Many of the reclamation projects under way today make use of recently developed and highly sophisticated treatment technologies. Yet these methods are not a prerequisite for, or necessarily the most desirable approach to water reuse. The physical, biological, and chemical treatments that today's engineers employ to purify water are replicating what nature can do if given the opportunity and the right environment. Many soils are excellent filters, straining from water unwanted particles and contaminants. Micro-organisms in the soil's upper layers thrive by decomposing organic matter, performing the biological treatment given sewage at most modern facilities. These actions, combined with a host of natural chemical processes in the soil, can often return wastewater to a remarkably high quality.

Though typically viewed as "pollutants," most wastewater constituents are nutrients that belong on the land, where they originated. Farmers and gardeners spend millions of dollars on fertilizers to give their crops the nitrogen, potassium, and phosphorus that urban wastewater contains in large amounts. According to one calculation, it would take 53 million barrels of oil—worth $1.4 billion—to replace with petroleum-based fertilizers the amount of nutrients yearly disposed of in U.S. wastewaters. Such payoffs are powerful incentives for this approach to water reuse. Would-be pollutants become valuable fertilizing agents; the irrigated land returns benefits, such as revenue from marketable crops, or a green landscape for a park; and the reclaimed water is a reliable, nearby source of supply.[63]

Most land-treatment systems are variants on a common design. Sewage is piped from a city's wastewater collectors to a series of lagoons, where it is biologically treated by bacteria and the air. Storage ponds hold the water so that it can be applied to the land at desired times, and also provide a safety buffer in case the water inadvertently becomes contaminated with a harmful pollutant. The remaining treatment takes place as the water percolates through the soil. The purified water can then recharge an underlying aquifer, or be collected for direct reuse. Especially in dry climates, a principal drawback is that a substantial share of water may evaporate from the storage and percolation basins, and the water's concentration of dissolved solids may increase. Planners must carefully compare the costs of land treatment with those of other reuse options, such as recharging groundwater through injection wells.

In their book, *Future Water*, John R. Sheaffer and Leonard A. Stevens cite some impressive successes with land-treatment designs. For example, one system that has been serving Muskegan County, Michigan, for a decade (and which author Sheaffer codesigned), handles 159,000 cubic meters of wastewater per day and irrigates 2,145 hectares of cropland. In 1981, the county earned $1.2 million by selling wastewater-irrigated corn for feed, and the treatment system turned a $250,000 profit.[64]

Land treatment was among the methods given special financial incentives by the 1977 U.S. Clean Water Act. By 1982, such systems were operating in at least 1,280 communities, four-fifths of which were irrigating crops. Between 1972 and 1982, an average of 71 new land treatment designs began operating each year, compared with an annual average of 17 between 1962 and 1972. Yet federal reuse specialist Richard E. Thomas says that the shift to water reuse is slow because "changes in the sanitary engineering curriculum at universities have been modest and consultants trained in the traditional treat and discharge concepts remain reluctant to plan, design, and implement reuse projects."[65]

Along with such institutional constraints, incomplete knowledge of the health effects of various pollutants remains a barrier to water reuse. Ways to reduce and monitor levels of bacteria in wastewater are well understood, but much is unknown about viruses, heavy metals, and organic chemicals. Where wastewater is used for irrigation or is otherwise applied to the land, crops must be selected carefully. Not only do they differ in their ability to take up nitrogen, phosphorus, and potassium—and thus to adequately treat the water—but some are harmed by, or may concentrate heavy metals,

such as cadmium, copper, nickel, and zinc. Unless removed, heavy
metals could accumulate in the soil or percolate to groundwater,
possibly contaminating a community's drinking water supply.
Pathogenic organisms can survive biological (secondary-level) treatment, which is the maximum now required at most U.S. facilities.
Moreover, many community treatment plants do not consistently
operate properly, and sometimes fail to meet specified quality standards. Stricter enforcement of standards could eliminate many of
these risks and uncertainties. But where they persist, treated wastewater must be used cautiously, and only where human exposure to it
is limited.[66]

In very special circumstances, wastewater reclaimed to an excep-
tionally high quality may be used to supplement a city's drinking-
water supplies. Though expensive, the most advanced biological and
chemical treatment processes can virtually eliminate harmful patho-
gens and dangerous pollutants. Windhoek, Namibia, was the first
city to add reclaimed water to its public supply, and has been doing
so for more than a decade. In the United States, Denver, Colorado, is
operating a demonstration plant to study this idea. In the spring of
1985, El Paso, Texas, began injecting highly treated wastewater into
the aquifer used as its primary public water supply—the first such
project in the nation. Much should be learned in the coming years
from these pioneering efforts in water-short areas.[67]

Conservation in Cities

Since residential and other community water uses account for less
than a tenth of water withdrawals worldwide, one would think these
needs could easily be met. Yet urban demands are concentrated in
relatively small areas, and can easily strain the capacity of local water
sources. As cities grow, engineers must develop supplies at distant
and less desirable sites, and at ever higher costs. Providing water and
wastewater services is also capital-intensive. The reservoirs, canals,
pipes, sewers, and treatment plants that comprise a modern water
and wastewater system require vast amounts of money to build,
expand, operate, and maintain. Though demanding only a small

share of the world's water, urban areas face severe physical and financial constraints on adequately serving their residents.

Cities in industrial and developing countries face disparate sets of urban water problems. The challenge in the Third World is to develop and install affordable technologies to meet the basic water supply and sanitation needs of the millions of people who now lack them. As urban populations expand, this challenge becomes more and more formidable. Peru-based engineers Carl R. Bartone and Henry J. Salas write that "The explosive urbanization in the Latin American countries has given rise almost overnight to peripheral communities that severely strain the ability of water and sewage authorities to provide even minimal services."[68] Cities in the industrial world, on the other hand, face spiraling demands associated with affluence and growth— thirsty green lawns in sprawling suburban areas, swimming pools, additional cars to wash, and houses filled with water-intensive appliances. With increasing constraints on expanding their supplies, many cities will experience more frequent shortages if steps toward conservation and greater water efficiency are not taken.

A simple comparison of population growth with available water supplies spells trouble for some metropolitan areas. The population of Tucson, Arizona, is projected to triple by the year 2025. Now entirely dependent on groundwater, the city is meeting half its present demand by mining its aquifers. More than 307 million cubic meters of groundwater pumped each year are not replaced by recharge. In Mexico City, where water use already exceeds the renewable supply by a third, population is expected to climb from 17 million to 30 million by the end of the century. Even though the city doubled the volume of its developed water supply between 1960 and 1976, the amount available per person declined. Mexico City's water problems are especially intractable since its best new freshwater sources are some 1,200 meters lower in elevation, creating the need for vast amounts of costly pumping power.[69]

Similarly, Beijing, in China's water-short North Plain, has grown from about 2 million people in 1949 to over 9.2 million today. Population growth and rising living standards are expected to increase household demands fivefold by the end of the century. Groundwater levels are falling precipitously, and the city's two principal reservoirs were so low in May 1985 that the water company began drawing supplies from a nearby petrochemical plant's reservoir. A recent assessment of Beijing's water situation concludes that "the prospect for the city to have a stable, sustained, and adequate water supply for domestic and industrial use looks bleak. Unless remedial measures are taken immediately and implemented on a sustained basis, sooner or later the city will run out of water."[70]

Though these are glaring problems, hundreds of cities worldwide will have trouble providing the water services many urban dwellers have come to expect. The U.S. Congressional Budget Office (CBO) estimates that of the nation's 756 large urban water systems (those serving more than 50,000 people), 170 will need an additional water supply by 1990. Developing these new sources would require an investment of $2.5 billion to $3.1 billion annually between 1980 and 1990. New supplies are most needed in the Southeast, Southwest, and West, and the CBO estimates that these regions collectively may face an annual capital shortfall of $400 million to $500 million, even assuming up to a doubling of water rates. Capital is also needed to replace and rehabilitate existing water systems, especially in the Northeast, and to service new growth. To meet all these needs, the nation's large water suppliers would have to be investing an average of $6.3 billion to $9.1 billion annually throughout the eighties. The CBO projects that investment capital will fall short of these needs by $900 million to $1.2 billion, or about 13 percent.[71]

Urban wastewater systems in the United States face no easier financial future. According to the Environmental Protection Agency's 1984 assessment, capital requirements through the year 2000 for constructing treatment plants and sewer lines, repairing and replacing aging portions of wastewater systems, and generally complying with the requirements of the federal Clean Water Act will total $108.9 billion—an annual cost (assuming a 10 percent interest rate) of $13.9 billion. Under current policies, the federal government will pay about one-third of these wastewater treatment costs, with states and local governments responsible for the rest. For municipal water supplies, the federal government now contributes only $1 for every $11 invested by states and localities. Communities thus face a large challenge in supplying water and wastewater services to their residents over the coming decades.[72]

Residential per capita water use varies greatly among the world's cities and need not be taken as fixed in any given location. In many European countries, daily residential use per person is less than half the U.S. average of about 425 liters. Residents of West Germany and France, for example, use on average less than 150 liters daily, and those in Sweden and the United Kingdom use about 200 liters. Israel, not surprisingly, has one of the lowest per capita use rates for an industrialized country, just 135 liters per day. In the drier western regions of the United States, residential use is typically 50 percent greater than in the East, since much water is used for outdoor lawns and gardens. Including water delivered to small businesses and industries and that used for watering parks and other public functions, daily usage rates exceeding 1,000 liters per person are not uncommon in the West. But great variation exists even among western cities in close proximity. Largely because of its conservation efforts, Tucson, Arizona's per capita use is 40 percent less than that of nearby Phoenix.[73]

Conservation has many times pulled communities through short-term crises, such as drought-induced shortages. Putting conservation to work in meeting long-range water needs, however, is a relatively new idea. Planners have typically projected future water demands based on the historical rate of growth in per capita water use and the projected future population. They then plan to meet this estimated demand by drilling more wells or building new reservoirs, and expanding the capacity of their water and wastewater treatment plants. Rarely have planners focused on reducing demand as a way to balance the long-term supply/demand equation.

Only a few cities have broken the historical rise in per capita water use. Because of conservation and water reuse, Tucson, Arizona, now plans for a per capita level of freshwater use 25 percent lower than existed in the early seventies. Like most water systems, Tucson's was designed to meet the city's peak day demand. For most western cities, this occurs on one of the hottest days of summer, and can be 2-4 times greater than the year-round average daily demand. A mid-seventies study found that with peak demand nearing the system's capacity, if the city's growth and pattern of water use continued, $145 million would have to be invested by 1983 to drill more groundwater wells and build larger transmission pipes. Until that time, the policy of Tucson Water, the municipally-owned water utility, was like that of most water suppliers—to plan to meet projected demands by developing new water sources and expanding the supply system. But faced with such large capital costs, the city chose to shift its strategy from simply meeting the demand to managing it, and it set a goal of postponing the need for some 30 percent of projected new capital requirements.[74]

41

Hefty water price increases caused an initial dramatic drop in Tucson's per capita use between the middle and late seventies. In June 1977, the city initiated its "Beat the Peak" program, aimed at cutting outdoor water use. Each summer, residents are asked not to water more than every other day, and never between the hours of 4 p.m. and 8 p.m. Desert landscaping is promoted as a replacement for green lawns. Largely because of altered outdoor water use patterns, Tucson Water's peak day pumpage dropped by 26 percent in less than a decade—from nearly 568,000 cubic meters in 1976 to 420,000 cubic meters in 1984. Moreover, year-round average demand fell by 27 percent, to about 570 liters per person per day—still high by many nations' standards, but low for a western U.S. city. Besides helping to slow the depletion of its aquifers, Tucson's comparatively modest investment in conservation allowed it to defer $45 million in capital costs that would have been needed to meet an otherwise unmanaged demand.[75]

Though less widely acclaimed for its efforts, El Paso, Texas, also is actively pursuing conservation's potential. The city, among the fastest growing in the nation, gets most of its fresh water from an aquifer expected to be depleted in 30-60 years. While pursuing replacement sources, El Paso is working to extend the aquifer's useful life through conservation and by substituting more expensive, but renewable river supplies. Its efforts have reduced annual pumping from the aquifer by an estimated 74 million cubic meters, enough water to supply about 280,000 residents. Moreover, conservation has allowed planners to adjust the expected per person demand downward by 17 percent in their projections of future water supply needs.[76] Though El Paso's water problems remain among the most formidable in the country, conservation is doing much to slow the inevitable loss of the city's primary supply and to offer some breathing room while other long-term solutions are sought.

Conservation requires creativity; there is no ready-made package that will prove effective and economical for every community. But successful efforts to permanently curb per capita demand invariably include some combination of water-saving technologies, economic incentives, regulations, and consumer education. These measures are mutually inforcing, and they are most effective when implemented jointly. Higher water rates, for example, encourage consumers to install water-saving devices in their homes and apartments, and to opt for native landscaping when purchasing a new home. Education is crucial to gain support for conservation, and to make people aware of the easy and cost-effective ways they can save water.[77]

In many western U.S. cities, lawn and garden watering accounts for 40-50 percent of residential water use and contributes greatly to water utilities' high peak demands. Curbing outdoor use thus provides the best opportunity in dry climates to lessen the needed capacity of water supply systems. Besides Tucson, the state of California and several other cities, including Denver, Aurora, and Fort Collins, Colorado; and Austin and San Antonio, Texas, are actively promoting water-conserving landscaping. A key message they communicate is that many options exist besides the stereotypical desert landscape of cacti and succulents.[78]

Many water-using technologies, especially those adopted in the United States, were not designed with water efficiency in mind. A typical U.S. toilet—the biggest water user in the home—turns about 19 liters (5 gallons) of drinking-quality water into wastewater each time it is flushed. This is an extravagance few water and wastewater utilities will long be able to afford, and a needless waste of costly, high-quality water. For comparison, most toilets in West Germany work well with only 9 liters, and in Scandinavia, 6-liter toilets have been routine since 1975.[79]

In recent years, U.S. manufacturers have designed a variety of fixtures that can greatly reduce water used indoors. (See Table 8.) Substituting the most common water-saving varieties—many of which are now widely installed in western homes—for conventional U.S. models can reduce total household water use by a fifth. The extremely low-water-using fixtures available from some manufacturers cut existing levels by as much as 50-70 percent. A bill introduced into the California legislature in 1985 would require that by 1988 all toilets installed in new construction use no more than 5.7 liters per flush—less than half the current limit, and 70 percent less than toilets commonly found in eastern residences.[80]

In humid climates, where outdoor watering claims a smaller share of water system capacities, cutting indoor use can significantly stretch the capacity of existing reservoirs. East Coast U.S. cities forced to ration water in 1985, for example, could help avoid such drastic drops in reservoir levels in the future by setting water-appliance efficiency standards and retrofitting existing fixtures with inexpensive water-saving devices. Simply getting toilets to operate at 13 liters per flush, instead of the typical 19-26 liters, could cut total residential water use by at least 10 percent.

Since conserving water indoors also translates into reduced sewage flows, plans to expand wastewater treatment facilities can be delayed or scaled down in size, again reducing investment needs. One study for the California Department of Water Resources found, for example, that reducing household water use in both new and existing homes to the economically optimum level would cut statewide capital requirements for wastewater treatment by more than $200 million. Saving water also saves energy since less water needs to be pumped through the urban system—from source, to treatment plant, to homes, and finally to the wastewater plant. Direct energy costs account for about 20 percent of the total operating budgets of most water and wastewater utilities, so cutting the volume of flow can significantly lower utility costs.[81]

Rounding out conservation's benefits are energy savings in the home. Since about 15 percent of the total energy used in a typical household is for heating water, measures that save hot water can significantly

Table 8: Potential Water Savings with Available Water-Efficient Household Fixtures in the United States

Fixture	Water Use	Water Savings Over Conventional Fixtures
		(percent)
Toilets	(liters/use)	
Conventional	19	—
Common low-flush	13	32
Washdown	4	79
Air-assisted	2	89
Showerheads	(liters/minute)	
Conventional	19	—
Common low-flow	11	42
Flow-limiting	7	63
Air-assisted	2	89
Clothes Washers	(liters/use)	
Conventional	140	—
Wash recycle	100	29
Front-loading	80	43
Faucets	(liters/minute)	
Conventional	12	—
Common low-flow	10	17
Flow-limiting	6	50

Sources: Figures for common water-saving fixtures from Brown and Caldwell, *Residential Water Conservation Projects* (Washington, D.C.: U.S. Department of Housing and Urban Development, 1984). All others from Robert L. Siegrist, "Minimum-Flow Plumbing Fixtures," *Journal of the American Water Works Association*, July 1983.

lower energy costs. In most cases these energy savings pay back the cost of the water-conserving fixture within a few years at most. For example, simply installing a low-flow (11.4 liters per minute) show-

"Simply installing a low-flow showerhead
can lower the year's electricity bill
for a family with an electric
water heater by about $100."

erhead, which costs little more than a conventional one, can lower the year's electricity bill for an average family of four with an electric water heater by about $100.[82]

Besides encouraging their consumers to conserve, urban water suppliers can stretch existing supplies through improved management techniques. Water agencies in the Washington, D.C. metropolitan area have in recent years revealed the vast potential of innovative management as an alternative to developing costly new water sources. Projections had suggested that the safe yield of the area's supplies (the amount of water that can be withdrawn daily with a small risk of supply disruption) would fall 30 percent short of demand by the year 2000. The typical response would be to build new dams and reservoirs to avoid the shortfall, but the parties involved failed to agree on a dam construction strategy. Conditions worsened, and finally they decided to explore options for increasing the safe yield of existing reservoirs. They calculated that through a combination of measures—including a conservation-oriented rate structure, public education, improved hydrologic forecasting, new institutional arrangements for more efficiently operating the water-delivery network, a reallocation of some flood storage capacity to water supply, and the construction of one small dam—that existing reservoirs could meet the area's needs until the year 2030. Investing $250 million in new reservoirs—the previous recommendation—became unnecessary.[83]

Investing in leak detection and repair is one of the most universally cost-effective conservation measures urban suppliers can undertake. Especially in older or poorly maintained water systems, a large share of the supply often seeps out through broken pipes and other faults in the distribution network. Many major cities in Latin America, Asia, Europe, and the eastern United States are losing as much as 25-50 percent of their water supplies in this way. These are costly losses because this "unaccounted-for water" is secured, stored, treated, and distributed, but never reaches a billable customer.[84]

Except where leakage is extremely low, finding and fixing leaks will usually pay. In Vienna, Austria, such an effort returned to productive use 64,000 cubic meters per day—roughly enough to meet the household needs of 400,000 people—and allowed the city to postpone new capacity investments. In the Philippines capital of Manila, water losses from an aging and poorly maintained supply network were averaging 50 percent in the seventies. A 1983 pilot project cut water losses in one northern area by a fifth, and the city's goal is to reduce losses to less than 30 percent throughout the metropolitan area. The repairs are expected to salvage enough water to serve an additional 1 million people.[85] The California Department of Water Resources is offering $1.3 million in grants to selected water utilities for leak detection and repair programs. The Department estimates that over the first two years the program will recover 49 million cubic meters of water at an average cost of about $30 per 1,000 cubic meters, several times lower than the current cost of water from most urban suppliers.[86]

Though conservation and better management can benefit growing Third World cities, the more urgent need is to develop water and sanitation technologies that can improve health standards while requiring less water, energy, and financial resources than the conventional technologies used in the industrial world. Few Third World cities can afford to adopt the kinds of water-intensive practices used in the United States today. Supplying the projected population growth in most Latin American cities, for example, will require that levels of water use not rise much above their present range: 75-150 liters per person per day. Many intermediate technologies for urban sanitation exist between the simple pit latrine and the water-born piped sewage system. Ventilated and lined pit latrines, toilets that use only 3 liters, multi-house septic tanks, and waste stabilization ponds combined with systems for reusing treated wastewaters are all being studied in various projects in Latin America. The African nations of Tanzania, Zambia, Botswana, and Lesotho are each implementing low-cost urban sanitation programs, some aided by bilateral and multilateral lending agencies. Such projects can greatly contribute toward developing new models of affordable water and sanitation services.[87]

As incomes rise in the Third World, efficiency must be built into water-using fixtures and appliances. Residents of Beijing, China, now use an average of 145 liters per person daily, but some high-quality

"Technology alone cannot close
the growing gap between
regional demands and supplies."

apartments register levels between 300 and 450 liters. Certain tourist hotels equipped with modern Western facilities reportedly use water at the extraordinary rate of 2,000 liters per person per day.[88] Given Beijing's already tenuous water situation, a widespread increase in demand even approaching these higher levels would surely thwart the region's economic growth.

Balancing the Water Equation

Though the technical means exist to greatly increase water efficiency, technology alone cannot close the growing gap between regional demands and supplies. Farmers in Israel, the Texas High Plains, and other areas where physical or economic constraints have made conservation a necessity, have shown that irrigation efficiencies can be raised at least 20-30 percent with new technologies and better management practices. Industrial recycling, reuse, and residential conservation can greatly reduce demands in water-short urban areas, without limiting economic growth or diminishing living standards. But unless the policies, laws, and institutions that govern water use begin to foster efficiency rather than discourage it, projected water shortages will worsen.

Pricing policies that promote wastefulness still prevail in most countries. Many governments, for example, pay all or most of the capital costs for major irrigation projects. Even in the United States, where western agriculture is clearly overdeveloped, farmers supplied with water from federal projects pay on average only one-fifth of the water's true cost. A 1982 study by the U.S. Department of Agriculture found that nearly 80 percent of the water from federal Bureau of Reclamation projects was priced at $12 per 1,000 cubic meters (5 cents per 1,000 gallons) or less, too low to make most efficiency investments economical. These prices reflect the set of lenient repayment terms for irrigation projects that evolved earlier this century, including no charge for interest, repayment periods as long as 60 years, and use of an "ability to pay" criterion in determining the share of costs beneficiaries would bear.[89]

How farmers respond to water prices depends on such factors as their levels of income, water's share of total production costs, and the value of their crops. But in Third World and industrial countries alike, farmers invariably will irrigate more efficiently if charged more for water. A study in Mexico, for example, found that where charges increased with the amount of water used, irrigation efficiencies averaged 20 percent higher than where farmers paid a fixed fee unrelated to their usage.[90]

Water prices should reflect the cost of supplying the next increment of water—called the marginal or replacement cost—so that consumers get accurate signals about water's true value. Government policies to subsidize water obviously deviate from this economic tenet. But even most water utilities set charges to cover their yearly revenue requirements, which are based on historical average costs, not marginal costs. A 1983 analysis of water pricing in Tucson, Arizona, a U.S. city considered progressive in water pricing and conservation, suggested that an immediate rate increase of at least 58 percent was needed for water to be priced at its replacement cost—in this case, the cost of water from the federally-built Central Arizona Project. Yet in recent years the Tucson water utility has raised its rates by only 5-8 percent annually, only a slight increase over inflation. As industry analyst Loren Mellendorf points out, pricing water below its true cost is tantamount to accepting "an inability to meet tomorrow's demands."[91]

In most countries, the water rights and laws that shape patterns of water use are also biased against conservation. In many European countries and U.S. jurisdictions, the right to an allotted quantity of water may be lost if the full allotment is not "beneficially" used. Since conservation is typically not considered a beneficial use, farmers and other water consumers are encouraged to use their full entitlements— even if they could economically reduce their water use. Contractual arrangements may restrict beneficiaries of government projects from transferring water either to a different location or to serve a different function. If the savings from conservation cannot in some way be marketed, water users again have little incentive to invest in efficiency. Rather than buying water that a conserving farmer could profitably offer, new water consumers pressure state and federal governments to build more water supply projects, and water demands and costs incessantly rise.[92]

"Pricing water below its true cost
is tantamount to accepting
'an inability to meet tomorrow's demands.'"

A number of jurisdictions have acted to remove these barriers to efficiency, but institutions change slowly. In 1983, officials in New South Wales, Australia, adopted a plan allowing water transfers between irrigators, though it applied only for the 1983-84 irrigation season. In the United States, the state of California amended its water laws in 1979 to allow farmers and other water consumers to use less than their full water right without risking the loss of that right. This removes the conservation disincentive inherent in the "use it or lose it" principle of western water rights.[93]

With proper incentives and an ability to transfer conserved water, many prospective "water crises" could disappear. The Metropolitan Water District (MWD) in southern California, which indirectly supplies water to 12.6 million people, may lose up to half its annual diversions from the Colorado River when the Central Arizona Project increases deliveries to Arizona cities. The MWD has estimated that such a loss could cause its supplies to fall 14 percent short of demand by the year 2000, and has pushed for greater imports of water from northern California. East of the MWD's service area, farmers in the Imperial Irrigation District (IID) irrigate 200,000 hectares with highly subsidized water from a federal reclamation project. Studies have shown that the IID could conserve up to 500 million cubic meters of water annually—roughly the amount of Colorado River water that the MWD expects to lose. Unfortunately, the conservation measures that could achieve these savings are not economical at the low prices the farmers pay.[94]

A 1983 analysis by the Environmental Defense Fund suggests, however, that if the MWD paid for conservation in the irrigation district in return for the water thereby saved, both parties would gain. It shows that such a conservation/transfer scheme could supply the MWD with more water than each of two proposals to increase diversions from the North—at a marginal cost respectively 27 percent and 42 percent less. (See Table 9). Even the most expensive conservation scenario, which includes lining a major canal, has a marginal cost 11 percent lower than the least expensive dam and diversion option. By choosing the conservation alternative over conventional supply strategies, the MWD could save an estimated $710 million over 20 years. The IID recently retained a private firm, the Pasadena-based Parsons Corporation, to further study conservation's potential and the market for

Table 9: Estimated Cost of Water Supply and Conservation Alternatives, Southern California

Representative Alternatives	Annual Yield	Marginal Cost
	(thousand cubic meters)	(dollars/thousand cubic meters)
Conserve/Transfer Irrigation Water	370,200	545
Develop Groundwater Basins	236,900	575
Reclaim and Reuse Wastewater	299,500	648
Conserve/Transfer Irrigation Water[1]	493,600	665
Build Newville Reservoir/ Increase Diversions of Northern Water	271,500	750
Build Los Vaqueros Reservoir/ Increase Diversions of Northern Water	327,000	943

[1]Includes lining a major canal in addition to the measures comprising the first conservation alternative.

Source: Adapted from Robert Stavins, "Trading Conservation Investments for Water," The Environmental Defense Fund, Berkeley, California, March 1983.

conserved water. Whether carried out by a private company or the MWD itself, conservation investments appear a cost-effective way to balance supply and demand in southern California, and should be explored elsewhere.[95]

Large-scale water development in the Third World began several decades later than in most industrial countries and is much less extensive. Yet given the inordinate investment requirements to expand irrigation, and the growing problems of waterlogging and soil salinization, attention must already turn to raising the efficiency and

"Failure to address the inefficiency,
inequity, and unreliability of irrigation systems
will set back the momentum
in Third World food production."

productivity of existing systems. According to Sadiqul I. Bhuiyan of the International Rice Research Institute in Manila, failure to address the inefficiency, inequity, and unreliability of irrigation systems will set back the momentum in Third World food production. Throughout Southeast Asia, he points out, the share of irrigation project budgets devoted to operation and maintenance is diminishing. Project staff are inadequately trained and are not sufficiently accountable for the system to manage it responsibly. British irrigation specialist W.R. Rangeley echoes these concerns, suggesting the need for national or international training programs in irrigation management.[96]

Over the past quarter century, groundwater use has burgeoned in many parts of the world, often proving a less expensive and more controllable supply for irrigation than surface water. Between 1960 and 1980, the Chinese constructed more than 2 million tubewells in the North Plain; the number privately installed in the Indus Plains of Pakistan rose from less than 5,000 to 200,000, and an estimated 2 million more are operating in India's Gangetic Plain. In areas such as these, where aquifers are at relatively shallow depths, seepage from surface canals adds to the supply underground. Recapturing this water through groundwater wells effectively increases the irrigation supply, and can also prevent the water table from rising and water-logging the root zone. So far few, if any, regions have developed the strategies and institutions needed to jointly manage groundwater and surface water effectively, despite potentially large benefits. World Bank economist Gerald T. O'Mara cites estimates that such management could increase output in Pakistan by 20 percent, and in China's North Plain, could reduce diversions from the Huang He (Yellow River) by 72 percent.[97]

Without adequate monitoring and regulation, intensive groundwater development can lead to aquifer depletion, falling water tables, land subsidence, and saltwater intrusion. The pervasiveness of these problems is a clear sign that existing institutions fail to foster sustainable groundwater use. Of the 122 billion cubic meters pumped from the U.S. groundwater supply each year, 26 billion—one-fifth—are non-renewable.[98] Those pumping this water pay only the private costs of their water use, not the public costs. They are charged nothing for the right to deplete a water reserve, even though such depletion diminishes the nation's future food and water security. Placing a tax on groundwater pumping wherever aquifers are being depleted would help equate private and social costs, and encourage conservation. Similarly, where water tables are dropping, taxing or otherwise limiting withdrawals can restore a balance between pumping and recharge.

A model attempt to balance water budgets in the United States is Arizona's 1980 Groundwater Management Act. It calls for each of the state's four most critical areas of groundwater overdraft to develop strategies to reduce groundwater pumping to the level of recharge by the year 2025. It requires conservation, calls for taxes on groundwater withdrawals, and, if it appears by the year 2006 that balance will not be achieved, allows the state to begin buying and retiring farmland. Projections for both the Phoenix and Tucson "Active Management Areas" (AMAs) show that most of the balancing will come from shifting water out of agriculture to supply urban and industrial growth. While the Phoenix population is projected to grow at an average rate exceeding 4 percent per year throughout the planning horizon, irrigated acreage is projected to drop an average of 1.3 percent annually. Similarly, population in the Tucson AMA is projected to more than triple by 2025, while agriculture's share of water withdrawals steadily drops. Whether the Act's goals can be achieved without limiting the burgeoning populations of these cities remains to be seen.[99]

Standards can help foster efficiency when the market fails to do so, or where water is critically scarce. In Israel, for example, which is now using virtually all of its available supplies, each farm, factory, and home is allotted only the minimum amount of water necessary, assuming up-to-date conservation measures are in place. As new technologies are developed, more stringent water use standards are set, ensuring that water efficiency continually increases. Several U.S. states now have laws requiring that fixtures installed in new homes, apartments, and offices meet specified water efficiency standards. But this transition could be greatly expanded—and made more quickly and uniformly—if standards were set at the federal level. The government set similar standards in the mid-seventies to boost auto fuel economy, and new cars are now 70 percent more fuel-efficient

"Placing a tax on groundwater pumping
wherever aquifers are being depleted
would help equate private and
social costs, and encourage conservation."

than the average car on the road a decade ago. If even modest water-efficiency standards were set for toilets, showerheads, faucets, and dishwashers, residential water demands by the year 2000 could be reduced by 1.5 billion cubic meters annually—a volume that would meet the yearly residential needs of nearly 10 million people.[100]

53

Planners facing projected water shortages should consider conservation and increased efficiency as alternatives to traditional water supply strategies. The Soviet Union has reportedly decided to proceed with a long-debated project to divert water from Siberian rivers into Soviet Central Asia. The project's main purpose is to expand irrigation, both to increase yields and to ensure greater output during dry years. With an estimated capital cost of $36.4 billion—or $15,700 for each of the 2.3 million hectares expected to come under irrigation—and uncalculated environmental risks, the diversion appears less desirable than a water efficiency strategy that could achieve the same goals.[101]

According to Soviet researchers, some 5 million hectares of irrigated land in Central Asia are badly in need of upgrading. Water withdrawals for these farms is excessive—often 2-3 times greater than those on experimental plots where irrigation systems have been modernized. Consequently, the output from each unit of water diverted to fields in the region is low. At $7,000 per hectare, modernizing all 5 million hectares would require an investment of $35 billion— roughly equal to that of the diversion. Yet the returns from such an investment would be far greater. Yields would increase, and land degradation from waterlogging and salinization would be greatly lessened. Just a 30 percent reduction in water withdrawals for those 5 million hectares—which modernization should achieve given the current high rates of water use Soviet researchers cite—could free as much water to expand irrigation as is proposed for the Siberian diversion, 25 billion cubic meters. Moreover, since these savings would begin to accrue in just a few years, farmers might bring new land under irrigation long before any water from Siberia would arrive.[102]

Writing in the journal *Soviet Geography*, reseachers from the Soviet Institute of Geography state, "There will obviously be a time when the water resources of the Aral Sea basin will be fully used up and water from Siberia will not yet be available . . . Until the arrival of Siberian water, southern Kazakhstan and Central Asia will have to rely on their own resources." They further state that the pace of reconstructing irrigation systems in the region is "obviously inadequate."[103] If the Soviet government cannot simultaneously invest in both the Siberian diversion and increasing water efficiency, the efficiency strategy—though institutionally more difficult to implement—appears the sounder choice.

In the United States, similar choices face the state of Texas, where depletion of the Ogallala Aquifer threatens the lucrative High Plains farming economy. With no action taken on long-standing, multibillion-dollar proposals to divert water into the region from distant rivers, Agriculture Commissioner Jim Hightower has proposed a strategy of state investments in water efficiency. By offering 10 percent purchase rebates, at a one-time cost to the state of $37 million, the plan would leverage the transition to more efficient irrigation methods on 1.3 million hectares of farmland. It reasonably assumes that farmers will buy cost-effective, water-conserving technologies, such as LEPA or surge units, if they are helped over the cash-flow hurdle. Including technical assistance and low-interest loans to stimulate other conservation investments, the complete plan would cut agricultural water use by an estimated 17 percent, or 2.46 billion cubic meters per year. This is 30 percent *more* water than would be supplied by a $10 billion cross-Texas diversion scheme examined by the Army Corps of Engineers. As Hightower says, "we can generate more water resources for much less money by making an investment in water conservation."[104]

High costs, environmental risks, and tight budgets will make large water projects increasingly unattractive and hard to implement for some time to come. Yet few officials and water managers have replaced their strategies of increasing supplies with ones geared toward reducing demand. This gap in policy, planning, and commitment can only lead to worsening water deficits and economic disruption. The transition to a water-efficient economy will not be easy or painless. But it has begun, and it should be fostered. With the technologies and methods now available, even modest expenditures on conservation and efficiency could make unnecessary many of the inordinately expensive, ecologically-disruptive water projects that have dominated water-planning agendas for decades.

Notes

1. Alfred G. Cuzen, "Appropriators Versus Expropriators: The Political Economy of Water in the West," in Terry L. Anderson, ed., *Water Rights: Scarce Resource Allocation, Bureaucracy, and the Environment* (San Francisco: Pacific Institute for Public Policy Research, 1983). Number of dams and projects from U.S. Congressional Budget Office, *Efficient Investments in Water Resources: Issues and Options* (Washington, D.C.: U.S. Government Printing Office, 1983).

2. Water level declines from Gordon Sloggett, *Prospects for Ground-Water Irrigation: Declining Levels and Rising Energy Costs* (Washington, D.C.: U.S. Department of Agriculture, 1981). Change in irrigated area from U.S. Department of Agriculture, *Agricultural Statistics 1983* (Washington, D.C.: U.S. Government Printing Office, 1983) and U.S. Bureau of the Census, "1982 Census of Agriculture," U.S. Department of Commerce, Washington, D.C., 1984.

3. Edwin D. Gutentag et al., *Geohydrology of the High Plains Aquifer in Parts of Colorado, Kansas, Nebraska, New Mexico, Oklahoma, South Dakota, Texas, and Wyoming*, U.S. Geological Survey Paper 1400-B (Washington, D.C.: U.S. Government Printing Office, 1984).

4. M.I. L'vovich and I.D. Tsigel'naya, "The Potential for Long-Term Regulation of Runoff in the Mountains of the Aral Sea Drainage Basin," *Soviet Geography*, October 1981; V.N. Bortnik, "Present and Predicted Changes in the Hydrological, Hydrochemical, and Hydrobiological Conditions of the Aral Sea," *Water Resources*, July 1984, translated from *Vodnye Resursy*, September-October 1983; Vaclav Smil, *The Bad Earth: Environmental Degradation in China* (Armonk, New York: M.E. Sharpe, Inc., 1984).

5. For a more thorough discussion of emerging water problems, see Sandra Postel, *Water: Rethinking Management in an Age of Scarcity* (Washington, D.C.: Worldwatch Institute, 1984). Water rationing from Donald Janson, "Kean Adds Restrictions on Water Use in Jersey," *New York Times*, May 17, 1985; Wayne King, "Severe Drought Hits Southwest," *New York Times*, June 6, 1984, "Managua to Ration Water," *New York Times*, December 20, 1984, and Deng Shulin, "Tianjin—the City that Needed Water," *China Reconstructs*, February 1982. Kenya's population growth from "1985 World Population Data Sheet," Population Reference Bureau, Inc., Washington, D.C.

6. U.S. Congressional Budget Office, *Efficient Investments in Water Resources*. See also Gilbert F. White, "Water Resource Adequacy: Illusion and Reality," in Julian Simon and Herman Kahn, eds., *The Resourceful Earth* (New York: Basil Blackwell, Inc., 1984).

7. High Plains Associates, *Six-State High Plains Ogallala Aquifer Regional Resources Study*, a report to the U.S. Department of Commerce and the High Plains Study Council (Austin, Tex.: 1982).

8. Yao Bangyi and Chen Qinglian, "South-North Water Transfer Project Plans," in Asit K. Biswas et al., eds., *Long-Distance Water Transfer* (Dublin: Tycooly International Publishing Ltd., 1983); G.V. Voropayev et al., "The Problem of Redistribution of Water Resources in the Midlands Region of the USSR," *Soviet Geography*, December 1983; Philip P. Micklin, "The Vast Diversion of Soviet Rivers," *Environment*, March 1985.

9. Bangyi and Qinglian, "South-North Water Transfer Project Plans."

10. Gordon Sloggett, *Energy and U.S. Agriculture: Irrigation Pumping, 1974-80* (Washington, D.C.: U.S. Department of Agriculture, 1982).

11. Water level decline from U.S. Geological Survey, *National Water Summary 1984* (Washington, D.C.: U.S. Government Printing Office, 1985). Decline in irrigated area from Comer Tuck, Texas Department of Water Resources, Austin, Texas, private communication, July 10, 1985.

12. Bortnik, "Present and Predicted Changes in the Hydrological Conditions of the Aral Sea"; Micklin, "Diversion of Soviet Rivers"; U.S. Water Resources Council, *The Nation's Water Resources 1975-2000*, Vol. 3, Analytical Data Summary (Washington, D.C.: U.S. Government Printing Office, 1978). Forty percent figure from David Pimentel et al., "Water Resources in Food and Energy Production," *Bioscience*, December 1982.

13. V.A. Kovda, "Loss of Productive Land due to Salinization," *Ambio*, Vol. 12, No. 2, 1983.

14. U.S. water use from Wayne B. Solley et al., *Estimated Use of Water in the United States in 1980* (Alexandria, Va.: U.S. Geological Survey, 1983).

15. Irrigated area from W.R. Rangeley, "Irrigation and Drainage in the World," paper presented at the International Conference on Food and Water, College Station, Texas," May 26-30, 1985.

16. Efficiency estimate from Rangeley, "Irrigation and Drainage in the World"; see Mohamed T. El-Ashry et al., "Salinity Pollution from Irrigated Agriculture," *Journal of Soil and Water Conservation*, January-February 1985.

17. Rangeley, "Irrigation and Drainage in the World."

18. For a good overview of irrigation efficiency, see E.G. Kruse and D.F. Heermann, "Implications of Irrigation System Efficiencies," *Journal of Soil and Water Conservation*, November-December 1977.

19. Wayne Clyma et al., *Land Leveling*, Planning Guide No. 1, Water Management Synthesis Project, prepared in cooperation with U.S. Agency for International Development, Fort Collins, Colorado, July 1981; California Department of Water Resources, *Water Conservation in California* (Sacramento, Calif.: California Resources Agency, 1984).

20. Sloggett, *Energy and U.S. Agriculture*; Gerald D. Knutson et al., "Cutting Energy Costs for Pumping Irrigation Water," Division of Agricultural Sciences, University of California, Berkeley, California, February 1981.

21. Kenneth Carver, Assistant Manager, High Plains Underground Water Conservation District No. 1, Lubbock, Texas, private communication, March 25, 1985; "Surge Improves Crop Uniformity," and "Surge Irrigation Catching On," *The Cross Section*, newsletter of the High Plains Underground Water Conservation District No. 1, Lubbock, Texas, November 1984. Payback from Tuck, private communication.

22. For background on sprinkler and other irrigation systems, see Kenneth D. Frederick and James C. Hanson, *Water for Western Agriculture* (Washington, D.C.: Resources for the Future, 1982). U.S. sprinkler irrigation trends from "1983 Irrigation Survey," *Irrigation Journal*, 1983, and "Irrigation Age Market Research Report," The Webb Company, St. Paul, Minnesota, 1983. Saudi Arabian citation from "Saudis Convert Oil to Water and Food," *The Groundwater Newsletter*, February 28, 1985.

23. Conventional sprinkler efficiency from Kruse and Heerman, "Implications of Irrigation System Efficiencies." For discussion of LEPA, see William M. Lyle, "Water Saving Techniques," in *Hope for the High Plains*, Proceedings of the Twenty-Seventh Annual New Mexico Water Conference, New Mexico Water Resources Research Institute, Las Cruces, New Mexico, April 1982.

24. Carver, private communication; Tuck, private communication. Use in Australia and Israel from Michael Courtney, "A Promising Breakthrough," *Quest*, Spring 1985. Water-saving calculation based on estimated savings of 3-4 acre-inches per acre in Office of Natural Resources, "Water Program for Texas Agriculture," Department of Agriculture, Austin, Texas, December, 1984, and center-pivot irrigated area from "Irrigation Age Market Research Report."

25. Background and basic features of drip irrigation from Kobe Shoji, "Drip Irrigation," *Scientific American*, November 1977. See also Sterling Davis and Dale Bucks, "Drip Irrigation," in Claude H. Pair et al., eds., *Irrigation* (Silver Spring, Md.: The Irrigation Association, 1983). Estimated water savings from J.S. Abbott, "Micro Irrigation—World Wide Usage," *ICID Bulletin*, January 1984.

26. Israel's efficiency gains from "Israel's Water Policy: A National Commitment," in Office of Technology Assessment, *Water Related Technologies for Sustainable Agriculture in Arid/Semiarid Lands: Selected Foreign Experience* (Washington, D.C.: U.S. Government Printing Office, 1983). 1983 U.S. drip area from "1983 Irrigation Survey." Current area worldwide from Abbott, "Micro Irrigation," plus known increases in the United States from the "1983 Irrigation Survey," and in Israel from Y. Kahana, private communication, Israel Ministry of Agriculture, Water Commission, Tel Aviv, Israel, April 28, 1985.

27. Costs from Paul Wilson et al., *Drip Irrigation for Cotton: Implications for Farm Profits* (Washington, D.C.: U.S. Department of Agriculture, 1984). Arizona acreage from Dale A. Bucks, U.S. Water Conservation Laboratory, Phoenix, Arizona, private communication, March 23, 1985. Area in Israel from Kahana, private communication. Area in Soviet Union from Abbott, "Micro Irrigation."

28. National Academy of Sciences, *More Water for Arid Lands: Promising Technologies and Research Opportunities* (Washington, D.C.: 1974); Christiaan Gischler and C. Fernandez Jauregui, "Low-Cost Techniques for Water Conservation and Management in Latin America," *Nature and Resources*, July-September 1984.

29. Investment cost from Rangeley, "Irrigation and Drainage in the World"; World Bank, *World Development Report 1983* (Washington, D.C.: 1983).

30. J. Alwis et al., *The Rajangana Irrigation Scheme, Sri Lanka: 1982 Diagnostic Analysis*, prepared in cooperation with the U.S. Agency for International Development, Water Management Synthesis project, Report No. 19, Colorado State University, Fort Collins, Colorado, December 1983.

31. Robert Chambers, "Food and Water as if People Mattered: A Professional Revolution," paper presented at the International Conference on Food and Water.

32. See California Department of Water Resources, *Water Conservation in California*. For a more technical discussion, see Edward A. Hiler and Terry A.

Howell, "Irrigation Options to Avoid Critical Stress: An Overview," in H.M. Taylor et al., *Limitations to Efficient Water Use in Crop Production* (Madison, Wisc.: American Society of Agronomy, 1983).

33. Cost figures from "Comparing Moisture Sensors," *The Cross Section*, September 1983. Test results and tomato grower estimate from Gail Richardson, *Saving Water from the Ground Up* (New York: INFORM, Inc., 1985).

34. Scheduling program in Nebraska from Paul E. Fischbach, "Irrigation Management (Scheduling) Application," in *Irrigation Challenges of the '80s* (St. Joseph, Mich.: American Society of Agricultural Engineers, 1981); California Department of Water Resources, *Water Conservation in California*; Michigan efforts from Leslie McConkey, "Irrigating the Water Wonderworld," *Futures*, Spring 1983.

35. Gaston Mahave and Jorge Dominguez, "Experiments at Farm Level to Introduce Technology in Irrigation: Its Influence on Production and Water Resources," in Brazilian National Committee, *Transactions of the 1st Regional Pan-American Conference*, Vol. 1, Salvador (Bahia), Brazil, October 1984.

36. Irrigation costs from Rangeley, "Irrigation and Drainage in the World."

37. B.A. Stewart and Earl Burnett, "Water Conservation Technology in Rainfed and Dryland Agriculture," paper presented at the International Conference on Food and Water.

38. Stewart and Burnett, "Water Conservation Technology in Rainfed and Dryland Agriculture."

39. Robert S. Loomis, "Crop Manipulations for Efficient Use of Water: An Overview," in Taylor et al., *Limitations to Efficient Water Use in Crop Production*.

40. Paul W. Unger and B.A. Stewart, "Soil Management for Efficient Water Use: An Overview," in Taylor et al., *Limitations to Efficient Water Use in Crop Production*. See also Jess Blair, "No-Till Trims Rising Debt Concern," *No-Till Farmer*, December 1984.

41. National Academy of Sciences, *More Water for Arid Lands*; United Nations Environment Programme, *Rain and Stormwater Harvesting in Rural Areas* (Dublin: Tycooly International Publishing Ltd., 1983).

42. Ibid. See Lester R. Brown and Edward C. Wolf, *Reversing Africa's Decline* (Washington, D.C.: Worldwatch Institute, 1985).

43. Texas Water Resources Institute and the Texas Agricultural Experiment Station, "Storing Soil Moisture," *Water Currents*, Fall 1984.

44. Loyd Stone, Department of Agronomy, Kansas State University, Manhattan, Kansas, private communication, January 11, 1985.

45. "Sorghum's the One that Can Take the Heat," *Farmline*, February 1985; Dirck Steimel, "Milo: A Grain of the Future?" *The Journal of Commerce*, August 21, 1984; Stone, private communication. Quote from Philip M. Raup, "Competition for Land and the Future of American Agriculture," in Sandra S. Batie and Robert G. Healy, *The Future of Agriculture as a Strategic Resource* (Washington, D.C.: The Conservation Foundation, 1980).

46. J. Doorenbos and A.H. Kassam, *Yield Response to Water* (Rome: U.N. Food and Agriculture Organization, 1979).

47. Edward A. Hiler and Terry A. Howell, "Irrigation Options to Avoid Critical Stress."

48. Doorenbos and Kassam, *Yield Response to Water*; M.A. Kahn et al., "Development of Supplies & Sanitation in Saudi Arabia," *African Technical Review*, June 1984.

49. Carl N. Hodges and Wayne L. Collins, "Future Food Production: The Potential is Infinite, the Reality May Not Be," *Proceedings of the American Philosophical Society*, Vol. 128, No. 1, 1984; James W. O'Leary, "The Role of Halophytes in Irrigated Agriculture," in Richard C. Staples, ed., *Salinity Tolerance in Plants: Strategies for Crop Improvement* (New York: John Wiley & Sons, Inc., 1984).

50. National Research Council, *Amaranth: Modern Prospects for an Ancient Crop* (Washington, D.C.: National Academy Press, 1984); C.S. Kauffman, *Amaranth Grain Production Guide 1984* (Emmaus, Pa.: Rodale Press, Inc., 1984); Wayne W. Applegate, Post Rock Natural Grains, Luray, Kansas, private communication, February 19, 1985; Charles D. McNeal, Paradise, Kansas, private communication, February 5, 1985; David Pimentel, Ithaca, New York, private communication, June 6, 1985.

51. Culp et al., *Water Reuse and Recycling: Evaluation of Needs and Potential*, Vol. 1 (Washington, D.C.: U.S. Department of the Interior, 1979); Ronald J. Turner, "Examining the Opportunities for Recycle and Reuse of Chemical Industry Wastewaters," in *Proceedings of the Water Reuse Symposium II*, Vol. 1 (Denver, Colo.: AWWA Research Foundation, 1981).

52. Armco example cited in Hamilton, "What Will We do When the Well Runs Dry?" *Harvard Business Review*, November-December 1984; L. Rakosh, "Water Reuse in the American Israeli Paper Mills, Hadera," in *Israqua '78* (Tel Aviv: Israel Centre of Waterworks Appliances, 1978). Soviet citation from Yu P. Belichenko and T.L. Dolgopolova, "Creation of Closed Water Management Systems at Industrial Enterprises," *Water Resources*, July 1984, translated from original article in *Vodnye Resursy*, January 1982.

53. Sandra Gay Yulke et al., "Water Reuse in the Pulp and Paper Industry in California," in *Water Reuse Symposium II*.

54. Yulke et al., "Water Reuse in the Pulp and Paper Industry." For other examples, see Leonard B. Antosiak and Charles A. Job, "Industrial Water Conservation Within the Great Lakes Region: An Overview," *Journal AWWA*, January 1981.

55. Swedish Preparatory Committee for the U.N. Water Conference, *Water in Sweden* (Stockholm: Ministry of Agriculture, 1977).

56. S. Arlosoroff, "Policy and Means for the Achievement of Efficient Water Use in Israel," in *Israqua '78*. Industrial norms cited in Nina Selbst, "Water Management in Israel," paper presented at 1 Congreso Nacional de Derecho de Aguas, Murcia, Spain, May 1982.

57. Gaston Mendoza Gamez and Francisco Flores Herrera, "Mexico City's Master Plan for Reuse," in *Water Reuse Symposium II*.

58. Selbst, "Water Management in Israel"; Aaron Meron, "Experience with Israel's Reclamation Systems," in *Future of Water Reuse: Proceedings of the Water Reuse Symposium III*, Vol. 1 (Denver, Colo.: AWWA Research Foundation, 1985).

59. L. Kettler, "Wastewater No Longer Is: Reclaimed Water Has Wide Range of Uses," *Water & Irrigation Review*, April 1981; Meron, "Experience with Israel's Reclamation Systems"; Emanuel Idelovitch, "Wastewater Reuse By Biological-Chemical Treatment and Groundwater Recharge," presented at the 50th Conference of the Water Pollution Control Federation, Philadelphia, Pennsylvania, October 1977. Projected ultimate reuse from Hillel I. Shuval, "The Development of the Wastewater Reuse Program in Israel," in *Water Reuse Symposium II*.

60. Culp et al., *Water Reuse and Recycling*.

61

61. James Crook, "Water Reuse in California," and Kenneth W. Willis, "The Future of Water Reclamation in California, in *Future of Water Reuse.*

62. State Water Project expansions from California Department of Water Resources, *State Water Project--Status of Water Conservation and Water Supply Augmentation Plans* (Sacramento: California Resources Agency, 1981). Reuse potential from California Department of Water Resources, *The California Water Plan: Projected Use and Available Water Supplies to 2010*; Robert Stavins, "Trading Conservation Investments for Water," The Environmental Defense Fund, San Francisco, California, 1983.

63. Calculation presented in John R. Sheaffer and Leonard A. Stevens, *Future Water* (New York: William Morrow and Company, Inc., 1983). For a brief discussion of these ideas, see John R. Sheaffer, "Circular vs. Linear Water Systems: Going Back to Nature's Way," *Environment*, October 1984.

64. Sheaffer and Stevens, *Future Water.*

65. Richard E. Thomas, "Reuse Due to Federal Wastewater Construction Grants," in *Future of Water Reuse.*

66. Charles P. Gerba et al., "Virus Removal During Land Application of Wastewater: Comparison of Three Projects," in *Future of Water Reuse*; Crook, "Water Reuse in California"; John F. Donovan and John E. Bates, *Guidelines for Water Reuse* (Cincinnati, Ohio: U.S. Environmental Protection Agency, 1980).

67. D.E. Bourne and G.S. Watermeyer, "Proposed Potable Reuse—An Epidemiological Study in Cape Town," in *Water Reuse Symposium II*; William C. Lauer et al., "Denver's Potable Water Reuse Project: Current Status," in *Future of Water Reuse*; Lee Wilson & Associates, "Water Supply Alternatives for El Paso," prepared for El Paso Water Utilities Public Service Board, Santa Fe, New Mexico, November 1981; Lee Wilson, Lee Wilson & Associates, Santa Fe, New Mexico, private communication, June 1985.

68. Carl R. Bartone and Henry J. Salas, "Developing Alternative Approaches to Urban Wastewater Disposal in Latin America and the Caribbean," *Bulletin of the Pan American Health Organization*, Vol. 18, No. 4, 1984.

69. Arizona Department of Water Resources, "Proposed Management Plan: First Management Period 1980-1990," Tucson Active Management Area, 1984; Mexico City figures from "Cities Athirst," *UNESCO Courier*, January 1985, and "Mexico City getting more potable water," *IDB News*, February 1985.

70. Quote from Laurence J.C. Ma and Liu Changming, "Water Resources Development and Its Environmental Impact in Beijing," *China Geographer*, No. 12, 1985. Water company actions from "Water Shortages Plague 188 Cities," *China Daily*, May 23, 1985.

71. U.S. Congressional Budget Office, *Public Works Infrastructure: Policy Considerations for the 1980's* (Washington, D.C.: U.S. Government Printing Office, 1983).

72. U.S. Environmental Protection Agency and Roy F. Weston, Inc., *1984 Needs Survey: Report to Congress* (Washington, D.C.: U.S. Environmental Protection Agency, 1984). Ratio from U.S. Congressional Budget Office, *Public Works Infrastructure*.

73. U.S. water use from Solley et al., *Estimated Use of Water in the United States in 1980*. Rates of water use for Europe cited in U.S. Congressional Budget Office, *Public Works Infrastructure*. Israeli use from Z. Golani and I. Ginzburg, "Advanced Means and Methods for Savings in Domestic Water Consumption," in *Israqua '78*. Comparison of Arizona cities from Tucson Water, "Energy Innovation through Applied Technology," Tucson, Arizona, 1984.

74. Tucson Water, "Conservation Programs," Tucson, Arizona, undated.

75. Tucson Water, "Conservation Programs"; Tucson Water, "Energy Innovation"; Janet Garcia, Tucson Water, Tucson, Arizona, private communication, April 19, 1985.

76. Lee Wilson & Associates, "Water Supply Alternatives for El Paso." Revised planning assumptions from Lee Wilson, Santa Fe, New Mexico, private communication, April 29, 1985.

77. See American Water Works Association, *Water Conservation Management* (Denver, Colo.: 1981).

78. "Water-Saving Plants Featured in 'X-Rated' Landscaping," *U.S. Water News*, December 1984.

79. West Germany reference from *World Environment Report*, April 4, 1984. Scandinavia reference from Robert L. Siegrist, "Minimum-Flow Plumbing Fixtures," *Journal AWWA*, July 1983.

80. Siegrist, "Minimum-Flow Plumbing Fixtures." California legislation from California Office of Water Conservation, "Legislative Update," *Water Conservation News*, June 1985.

81. Donald W. Lystra et al., "Energy Conservation Opportunities in Municipal Water and Wastewater Systems," *Journal AWWA*, April 1981. California study from Jimmy Koyasako, "Water Conservation and Wastewater Flow Reduction—Is It Worth It?" in Dynamac Corporation, ed., *Proceedings of the National Water Conservation Conference on Publicly Supplied Potable Water* (Washington, D.C.: U.S. Department of Commerce, 1982).

82. Estimate of savings from Brown and Caldwell, *Residential Water Conservation Projects* (Washington, D.C.: U.S. Department of Housing and Urban Development, 1984). The report assumes an electricity cost of 7 cents per kilowatt-hour.

83. Case is described in U.S. Geological Survey, *National Water Summary 1983--Hydrologic Events and Issues* (Washington, D.C.: U.S. Government Printing Office, 1984) and The Conservation Foundation, *State of the Environment: An Assessment at Mid-Decade* (Washington, D.C.: 1984).

84. See "Runaway Water: The Lost Resource," *World Water*, November 1983, and Fred Pearce and Mick Hamer, "The Empire's Last Stand," *New Scientist*, May 12, 1983.

85. Austria citation from F. Auzias "Economie d'Eau at Lutte contre le Gaspillage," *Aqua*, Vol. 5, 1983. Manila program described in "Leak Detectives Boost Manila Supply," *World Water*, November 1983.

86. Adrian Griffin and Christopher L. Carr, "An Examination of the Benefits of Leak Detection," paper presented to the American Water Works Association Annual Conference, Dallas, Texas, June 1984. Costs of municipal water from California Department of Water Resources, *Urban Water Use in California* (Sacramento: California Resources Agency, 1983).

87. Latin American usage rates from E. Glenn Wagner, "The Latin American Approach to Improving Water Supplies," *Journal AWWA*, April 1983. Latin American projects from Bartone and Salas, "Developing Alternative Approaches to Urban Wastewater Disposal. African programs from E.J. Schiller, "Water and Health in Africa," *Water International*, June 1984.

88. Ma and Changming, "Water Resources Development and Its Environmental Impact in Beijing."

89. Share paid by U.S. farmers from U.S. Congressional Budget Office, *Efficient Investments in Water Resources*; David L. Wilson and Harry W. Ayer, "The Cost of Water in Western Agriculture," Economic Research Service,

U.S. Department of Agriculture, July 1982. For historical background, see Gary Weatherford and Helen Ingram, "Legal-Institutional Limitations on Water Use," in Ernest A. Engelbert and Ann Foley Scheuring, eds., *Water Scarcity: Impacts on Western Agriculture* (Berkeley, Calif.: University of California Press, 1984).

90. Study described in United Nations, *Efficiency and Distributional Equity in the Use and Treatment of Water: Guidelines for Pricing and Regulations* (New York: United Nations, 1980).

91. William E. Martin et al., *Saving Water in a Desert City* (Washington, D.C.: Resources for the Future, 1984). Recent rate increases from Garcia, Tucson Water, private communication; Loren D. Mellendorf, "The Water Utility Industry and Its Problems," *Public Utilities Fortnightly*, March 17, 1983.

92. W.D. Watson et al., *Water 2000: Agricultural Water Demand and Issues* (Canberra: Australian Government Publishing Service, 1983); United Nations Economic Commission for Europe, *Policies and Strategies for Rational Use of Water in the ECE Region* (New York: United Nations, 1983); Gaylord V. Skogerboe and George E. Radosevich, "Future Water Development Policies," *Water Supply and Management*, Vol. 6, No. 2, 1982. For general discussion on water markets, see Terry L. Anderson, *The Water Crisis: Ending the Policy Drought* (Baltimore, Md.: The Johns Hopkins University Press, 1983).

93. Watson et al., *Water 2000: Agricultural Water Demand and Issues*; the California Department of Water Resources, *Water Conservation in California*.

94. The California Department of Water Resources, *Water Conservation in California*; Stavins, "Trading Conservation Investments for Water."

95. Stavins, "Trading Conservation Investments for Water"; Tony Profumo, Parsons Corporation, Pasadena, California, private communication, July, 1985.

96. Sadiqul I. Bhuiyan, "Water Technology for Food Production: Expectations and Realities in the Developing Countries," paper presented at the International Conference on Food and Water; Rangeley, "Irrigation and Drainage in the World." See also Michael Cross, "Irrigation's Role in Solving the Food Crisis," *New Scientist*, May 9, 1985.

97. Gerald T. O'Mara, *Issues in the Efficient Use of Surface and Groundwater in Irrigation* (Washington, D.C.: The World Bank, 1984).

98. Yearly groundwater use from Solley et al., *Estimated Use of Water in the*

United States. Depletion figures from U.S. Geological Survey, *National Wate Summary 1983.*

99. Projections from Arizona Department of Water Resources, "Proposec Management Plan: First Management Period 1980-1990," Phoenix Activ Management Area, 1984, and companion document for Tucson.

100. Estimated savings are for common water-efficient fixtures given i Brown and Caldwell, *Residential Water Conservation Projects.* Calculated sav ings assume that the entire increase in population between 1985 and the yea 2000 would be using the more efficient fixtures, as well as 15 percent of th existing population (because of remodeling, or purchases of new homes o new appliances). No attempt was made to discount for states with water efficient plumbing codes already in effect.

101. Diversion plans described in O.A. Kibal'chich and N.I. Koronkevich "Some of the Results and Tasks of Geographic Investigations on the Water Transfer Project," *Soviet Geography,* December 1983. Cost estimates from Philip M. Micklin, "Recent Developments in Large-Scale Water Transfers ir the USSR," *Soviet Geography,* April 1984.

102. Based on figures and discussion in A.S. Kes' et al., "The Present Stat and Future Prospects of Using Local Water Resources in Central Asia anc Southern Kazakhstan," *Soviet Geography,* June 1982.

103. Kes' et al., "Using Local Water Resources in Central Asia and Southerr Kazakhstan."

104. Office of Natural Resources, "Water Program for Texas Agriculture" Rick Piltz, Texas Office of Natural Resources, Austin, Texas, private commu nication, June 1985. Corps findings from High Plains Associates, *Six-Stat High Plains Ogallala Aquifer Regional Resources Study.* Quote from Jim High tower, "Incentive is Needed to Stretch Water Supply," *U.S. Water News* February 1985.

SANDRA POSTEL is a senior researcher with Worldwatch Institut and author of "Managing Freshwater Supplies" in *State of the Worl 1985* (W. W. Norton, 1985). Prior to joining Worldwatch, she was ; resource analyst with a California-based consulting firm where sh researched water issues. She has studied geology and political scienc at Wittenberg University and resource economics and policy at Duk University.

THE WORLDWATCH PAPER SERIES

No. of
Copies

1. **The Other Energy Crisis: Firewood** by Erik Eckholm.
2. **The Politics and Responsibility of the North American Breadbasket** by Lester R. Brown.
3. **Women in Politics: A Global Review** by Kathleen Newland.
4. **Energy: The Case for Conservation** by Denis Hayes.
5. **Twenty-two Dimensions of the Population Problem** by Lester R. Brown, Patricia L. McGrath, and Bruce Stokes.
6. **Nuclear Power: The Fifth Horseman** by Denis Hayes.
7. **The Unfinished Assignment: Equal Education for Women** by Patricia L. McGrath.
8. **World Population Trends: Signs of Hope, Signs of Stress** by Lester R. Brown.
9. **The Two Faces of Malnutrition** by Erik Eckholm and Frank Record.
10. **Health: The Family Planning Factor** by Erik Eckholm and Kathleen Newland.
11. **Energy: The Solar Prospect** by Denis Hayes.
12. **Filling The Family Planning Gap** by Bruce Stokes.
13. **Spreading Deserts—The Hand of Man** by Erik Eckholm and Lester R. Brown.
14. **Redefining National Security** by Lester R. Brown.
15. **Energy for Development: Third World Options** by Denis Hayes.
16. **Women and Population Growth: Choice Beyond Childbearing** by Kathleen Newland.
17. **Local Responses to Global Problems: A Key to Meeting Basic Human Needs** by Bruce Stokes.
18. **Cutting Tobacco's Toll** by Erik Eckholm.
19. **The Solar Energy Timetable** by Denis Hayes.
20. **The Global Economic Prospect: New Sources of Economic Stress** by Lester R. Brown.
21. **Soft Technologies, Hard Choices** by Colin Norman.
22. **Disappearing Species: The Social Challenge** by Erik Eckholm.
23. **Repairs, Reuse, Recycling—First Steps Toward a Sustainable Society** by Denis Hayes.
24. **The Worldwide Loss of Cropland** by Lester R. Brown.
25. **Worker Participation—Productivity and the Quality of Work Life** by Bruce Stokes.
26. **Planting for the Future: Forestry for Human Needs** by Erik Eckholm.
27. **Pollution: The Neglected Dimensions** by Denis Hayes.
28. **Global Employment and Economic Justice: The Policy Challenge** by Kathleen Newland.
29. **Resource Trends and Population Policy: A Time for Reassessment** by Lester R. Brown.
30. **The Dispossessed of the Earth: Land Reform and Sustainable Development** by Erik Eckholm.
31. **Knowledge and Power: The Global Research and Development Budget** by Colin Norman.
32. **The Future of the Automobile in an Oil-Short World** by Lester R. Brown, Christopher Flavin, and Colin Norman.
33. **International Migration: The Search for Work** by Kathleen Newland.
34. **Inflation: The Rising Cost of Living on a Small Planet** by Robert Fuller.
35. **Food or Fuel: New Competition for the World's Cropland** by Lester R. Brown.
36. **The Future of Synthetic Materials: The Petroleum Connection** by Christopher Flavin.
37. **Women, Men, and The Division of Labor** by Kathleen Newland.
38. **City Limits: Emerging Constraints on Urban Growth** by Kathleen Newland.

_____ **Total Copies**

Single Copy—$4.00

Bulk Copies (any combination of titles)
2-5: $3.00 each   6-20: $2.00 each   21 or more: $1.00 each

Calendar Year Subscription (1985 subscription begins with Paper 63)
U.S. $25.00 _____

Make check payable to Worldwatch Institute
1776 Massachusetts Avenue NW, Washington, D.C. 20036 USA

Enclosed is my check for U.S. $ _____

name _____

address _____

city _____   state _____   zip/country

486 TE BR 1304
4/15/96 39250